DATE DUE

M.H.C. OCT LIBRARY '72			
Int. Due Jan. 10, 1994			
NOV 07 '94 M.C. Library			
NOV 28 '94			
		DISCARD	
GAYLORD			PRINTED IN U.S.A.

Books by Barbara Habenstreit

CHANGING AMERICA AND THE SUPREME COURT

THE MAKING OF URBAN AMERICA

ETERNAL VIGILANCE: The American Civil Liberties Union in Action

ETERNAL VIGILANCE

The American Civil Liberties Union in Action
by Barbara Habenstreit

The ACLU is a non-profit, nationwide legal organization whose sole purpose is the protection and preservation of the Bill of Rights. It is not political. It does not take sides in election campaigns. Its only concern is to make sure that all Americans have the right to the maximum possible individual liberty. This is the dramatic story of the ACLU—how it was formed, its many distinguished founders and exciting case histories that show the kind of action it has taken to protect the freedom of all Americans.

Eternal Vigilance

The American Civil Liberties Union in Action

by Barbara Habenstreit

Andrew S. Thomas Memorial Library
MORRIS HARVEY COLLEGE, CHARLESTON, W. VA.

JULIAN MESSNER NEW YORK

79445

Published by Julian Messner
a division of Simon & Schuster, Inc.
1 West 39th Street, New York, N.Y. 10018
All Rights Reserved

Copyright, ©, 1971 by Barbara Habenstreit

342.73
H113e

Printed in the United States of America

ISBN 0-671-32447-0 Cloth Trade
      0-671-32448-9 MCE

Library of Congress Catalog Card No. 76-160310

ACKNOWLEDGEMENTS

I would like to thank Alan Reitman, Associate Director of the American Civil Liberties Union, and Johanna Roosevelt, ACLU Librarian, for their invaluable assistance in the preparation of this book. Most of the inforamtion came from ACLU legal files, press releases, newspapers, pamphlets and speeches, all of which may be found in the New York offices of the ACLU.

B.H.

"Eternal Vigilance is the price of liberty."
—Thomas Jefferson

CONTENTS

1	The Battle That Never Ends	9
2	When Johnny Refuses a Gun	27
3	Flags and Fanatics	51
4	White Liberals and Black Men	63
5	Speaking Out on the Far Right	83
6	Big Brother Is Watching You	99
7	The Right to Eat	119
8	A Bill of Rights for the Young	135
9	Helping the Oppressed: Women, the Mentally Ill, Homosexuals	151
10	The ACLU Today and Tomorrow	167
	The Bill of Rights	181
	Suggested Further Readings	183
	Index	185

[1]
THE BATTLE THAT NEVER ENDS

One evening in May 1970, a group of people were attending a reception at the home of David T. Lykken, a professor at the University of Minnesota. The purpose of the gathering was to raise money for an anti-war rally that was being planned for the near future.

The guests were milling about, discussing politics and nibbling on hors d'oeuvres, when the police suddenly burst into the house. They arrested Professor Lykken and charged him with running a "disorderly house." Eighteen of his guests were also arrested, including Matthew Stark, head of the Minnesota affiliate of the American Civil Liberties Union. They were charged with "frequenting a disorderly house" because Professor Lykken was allegedly selling liquor in his house without a license. The complaint against him had been lodged by a police undercover agent who had been attending the party as a "guest," and claimed to have bought a can of beer there for 50 cents.

In addition to making the arrests, 16 policemen searched Professor Lykken's home—without the required search warrant—and seized some files belonging to the Minnesota Civil Liberties Union, as well as professional and scientific papers, Parent-Teacher Association reports and other materials.

This full-scale police raid was certainly way out of proportion to the minor offense that was supposedly committed at the party. A great many other groups had held similar fund-raising parties where guests could get beer or hard liquor in return for a small contribution to "the cause"—whether the cause was charitable, social or political. This was not generally thought of as "selling" liquor, because no individual made a profit from it. Such parties had never seemed to bother the police before, so why did they suddenly storm into Professor Lykken's house? And, above all, why did they have an undercover agent there in the first place?

Lawyers from the Minnesota Civil Liberties Union, who defended Professor Lykken and his guests, argued in court that the real purpose of the police raid was to harass and intimidate citizens who held pro-peace and -civil liberties views. The court agreed, and the charges against the defendants were dropped. Thus, the police were prevented from overstepping their powers and harassing people whose views they disliked.

Such was a typical case from the files of the American Civil Liberties Union. Here, the ACLU was defending the right of peaceful assembly that is guaranteed to all Americans by the First Amendment of the United States Constitution. It was also defending the Fourth Amendment's guarantee that American people shall be "secure in their persons, houses, papers, and effects, against unreasonable searches and seizures."

The Lykken case was clearly a "civil liberties" case, involving violations of basic rights and freedoms that are protected by the first 10 Amendments to the Constitution (the Bill of Rights), plus the Fourteenth Amendment.

Not all civil liberties cases are so clear-cut, however. A few years earlier, the ACLU filed a friend-of-the-court brief in a case in Connecticut of an entirely different nature.

Connecticut had a law that banned the sale and use of all birth control devices. It was also a crime for anyone to dis-

The Battle That Never Ends

tribute information about these devices, which made it impossible for people in Connecticut to practice family-planning legally.

The law was on the books for many years until finally, in the late 1950s, several people got together to challenge it. Among them was a 25-year-old housewife who demanded the right to buy and use birth control devices because, she said, another pregnancy "would almost inevitably result in death." Other parties to the lawsuit included two couples whose previous babies had died. Neither couple wanted to risk further pregnancies, fearing that the anxiety and possible heartbreak that might occur could "result in permanent emotional imbalance." Another couple, a Yale instructor and his wife, wanted to postpone babies until they were financially able to support them. The last party to the lawsuit, a doctor who was chairman of the Obstetrics and Gynecology Department at Yale Medical School, challenged the law on the grounds that he had a professional obligation as a doctor to give advice about contraceptives.

The American Civil Liberties Union aided in this case, *Griswold vs. Connecticut,* and by 1965 had helped take it all the way up to the Supreme Court. The main argument was that the Connecticut law violated the people's right to privacy in their private relations.

But what provision of the Bill of Rights guarantees a "right of privacy"?

The answer, of course, is none. However, the ACLU argued that a right of privacy was *implied* throughout the Bill of Rights, and was a privilege reserved to the people by the Ninth and Tenth Amendments.

A divided Supreme Court upheld this argument, declaring Connecticut's ban on birth control devices unconstitutional.

Thus, for the first time, a "right of privacy" was read into the Constitution.

The two cases mentioned above were vastly different from each other, yet each involved a violation of civil liberties and so fell under the protective wing of the American Civil Liberties Union.

The ACLU is a non-profit, nationwide legal organization with headquarters in New York City in a massive, aging building on Manhattan's lower Fifth Avenue. In the rear of the building is an ancient elevator, which takes the visitor up to the ninth floor. Here, from a maze of cluttered rooms connected by long, narrow corridors, the ACLU wages its daily struggle to protect Americans' basic rights and freedoms.

There is an air of casualness about the place that contrasts sharply with most mid-Manhattan legal offices. Staff members amble about, some in bell-bottom jeans and beaded necklaces, others in business suits and ties, or fashionable dresses. There are spry, middle-aged ladies with bouffant hairdos working together with young men whose hair hangs loosely at shoulder length. Nobody dresses or looks quite like anybody else; nevertheless, a unity of spirit links these assorted individuals together. Early one afternoon in the spring of 1970, staff members were all busy at their jobs. In a room at the far end of a corridor, the faint sounds of a radio could be heard. Suddenly, a loud cheer bellowed from the room. Several people bounded out and raced around the corridors to shout the news to the rest of the staff: the Senate had just rejected President Nixon's nomination of G. Harrold Carswell to the Supreme Court.

Officially, the ACLU had followed its traditional policy of not supporting or opposing persons who were elected or appointed to public office. But Carswell, as a man and as a judge, offended many of the principles that the American Civil Liberties Union stood for. He had a careless disregard for individual liberties, and barely cloaked his dislike of the whole integration drive in the South. To those who shared the ACLU's ideals, Carswell was a natural enemy.

The brief, spontaneous celebration over his defeat was completely in keeping with the free-spirited atmosphere at ACLU headquarters. Work there always seems to go on in a haphazard way. Offices are cramped and messy; the library bulges with too many books for its shelves; legal files, papers and memos are strewn about everywhere in random disarray. The sight of a small brown dog (a staff member's pet) roaming freely through the hallways completes the picture.

But this air of nonchalance belies the difficult, painstaking legal work that is always going on there. Each year, the ACLU brings hundreds of civil liberties cases to court to advance its fundamental goal—the protection and preservation of the Bill of Rights.

The ACLU is not a political group. It does not take sides in election campaigns and it doesn't care at all about the politics of the people or groups it defends. Its only concern is to make sure that all Americans are free to say, write or read whatever they please; associate with anyone they want; receive fair and equal treatment before the law; and, in their private lives, simply to be let alone. As the ACLU Charter states, the group's "single purpose" is "defending the whole Bill of Rights for everyone."

This does not mean that everyone should be allowed to *do* exactly as he wishes. Each person's rights and freedoms are bounded by the rights and freedoms of others, and by the needs of the nation as a whole. As the old saying goes, "Your right to swing your fist ends where my nose begins." But within such broad limits, the ACLU believes, everyone has the right to the maximum possible individual liberty. "Liberty under law" is the byword.

The same is true regarding individual rights. For example, the ACLU would not concern itself with the guilt or innocence of a man on trial for murder, but it would care about whether or not he received all the legal protection he was entitled to under the Bill of Rights. The ACLU would want to know if the police had warned the man of his right to remain silent before coaxing a confession out of him. Or, in the case of a poor defendant, it might want to know if the court-appointed lawyer had defended him adequately. No matter how heinous the crime the man had committed, the ACLU would come to his aid if it felt he had been denied any of his fundamental legal rights.

It is this attitude that led the ACLU to come forward on behalf of Lt. William Calley, Jr., an army platoon leader who was accused of murdering more than 100 unarmed South Vietnamese women, children and old men in the war-torn hamlet of Mylai. When Calley was facing a court-martial, the ACLU urged the government to drop the charges against him because the publicity had made a fair trial impossible. Newspapers had already printed damaging statements by men who were going to be witnesses against Calley at the trial, and some of these men also might have incriminated themselves in the interviews, possibly resulting in their own prosecution later on. Because of these disclosures, plus the vivid press descriptions and photos of the Mylai massacre, the ACLU felt that Calley could not possibly receive a fair trial.

The Supreme Court had ruled several years earlier that pretrial "sensationalism" could reach such heights that it would be impossible to find jurors who were unaffected by the publicity. Because of this, the Court had overturned the conviction of Dr. Samuel Sheppard, a well-known osteopath who had been found guilty of murdering his wife. The ACLU felt that the same type of lurid publicity that had made Sheppard's trial unfair was also a factor in the Calley case.

In a letter to Defense Secretary Melvin Laird, the ACLU said that if the Army refused to drop the prosecution, the Union would attempt to enter the case on Calley's behalf.

On the other hand, the ACLU certainly did not want to have the newspapers censored in any way, and stated they must be free to print whatever they felt was newsworthy and appropriate. If not for a free press, the ACLU noted, the American people might never have found out about the Mylai massacre in the first place.

Trying to safeguard the legal rights of someone as notorious and controversial as Lt. Calley is typical of the kind of work the American Civil Liberties Union has been doing for more than 50 years. People like Calley, who may have committed unspeakable acts that arouse the nation's fury, are often in danger of having their rights trampled upon by an overzealous public.

Those who seriously offend the majority of Americans by their actions or beliefs—not only actual criminals, but political dissenters, religious non-conformists, social rebels or black militants— are more likely than others to have their legal rights violated. They may be prevented from speaking in public when they have every right to do so; they may not be able to send their literature through the mails; they may languish in jail for many months before trial because excessively high bail was set for them. In short, those whose beliefs and activities are outside the mainstream of American orthodoxy often come face to face with repression. They are the ones who are most in need of legal protection because all too often society tends to ignore their rights. The American Civil Liberties Union exists to help them, as well as anyone else who is denied the full protection of the Bill of Rights.

The ACLU was founded during a time when civil liberties were in great jeopardy—the World War I era. The nation was consumed with patriotic ardor then, and anyone who spoke out against the war or the government was treated very harshly. Dissenters were not tolerated—in fact, they were often tarred and feathered by angry mobs, or strung from flagpoles, or painted yellow—all in the name of patriotism.

In 1917, Congress passed the first espionage and sedition act since the days of John Adams. The following year, even more sweeping measures were passed against disloyal speech. It became a crime to utter "disloyal, profane, scurrilous or abrasive language" about the government, the Constitution, the armed forces, the uniform or the flag. It was also a criminal offense to make fun of any of them. Furthermore, the government could cut off all mail to and from anyone who violated these laws.

Such measures, approved by a Democratic Congress and President, practically made it a crime to criticize the administration. In this respect, they could even have been used to muffle the Republican Party; but in practice they were not.

Nevertheless, federal courts handed out severe sentences to individuals who violated these laws, such as 15 years in jail for speaking out against the draft; 10 years and a $1,000 fine for opposing the Liberty Bonds; 20 years and a $10,000 fine for calling the government a liar, predicting a German victory and applauding the sinking of an American ocean liner, *The Lusitania*.

The Socialist leader Eugene V. Debs was sentenced to 10

years in jail for telling an audience in an anti-war speech, "You need to know that you are fit for something better than slavery and cannon fodder." A woman named Rose Pastor Stokes wrote a letter to a St. Louis newspaper saying, "I am for the people and the government is for the profiteers." For this, she received a 10-year jail sentence.

From this climate of fear and repression, the American Civil Liberties Union was born. Formed in 1920, it vowed to protect the Bill of Rights in a nation so bent on "saving the world for democracy" that it was endangering its own democratic traditions.

Among the founders of the ACLU were people who would later be recognized as some of America's most distinguished citizens: Roger Baldwin, director of the ACLU for 30 years; Jane Addams, social worker and founder of the famous Chicago settlement, Hull House; Felix Frankfurter, who later became a justice of the Supreme Court; Clarence Darrow and Morris Ernst, who would soon become two of the best-known lawyers in the country; Norman Thomas, leader of the Socialist Party and frequent presidential candidate; John Dewey, the noted educator; and many other prominent Americans in various walks of life.

They set up the ACLU as a permanent, national non-partisan organization dedicated to preserving individual liberty. During the first decade of its existence, the ACLU spent most of its time defending labor leaders, socialists, communists and other radicals who were being denied such basic rights as freedom of speech and freedom of assembly. Because it defended so many radicals, the ACLU itself was frowned upon as a left-wing and possibly "subversive" group. The image lingered, and it was many years before the Union was finally accepted as "respectable."

During the 1920s, the ACLU also became involved in one of the most famous academic freedom cases in American history—the Scopes trial. Just as the government was suppressing political dissent, it was also stifling freedom to teach. Some states had laws that forbade the teaching of German or any language but English; other states had banned Karl Marx's works from the classrooms. When Tennessee forbade the teaching of Darwin's theory of evolution, the ACLU decided to challenge the ban. It offered to defend any teacher who was punished for revealing the forbidden theory to his students, and advertised in the Tennessee newspapers for volunteers. A young teacher from Dayton, John Thomas Scopes, stepped forward to help the ACLU test the law. When he was brought to trial, his whole defense was financed by the ACLU, which provided him with such outstanding lawyers as Clarence Darrow and Arthur Garfield Hays.

Although Scopes was found guilty and the law was upheld, the sensational trial forced Americans to wake up to what was happening in the classrooms.

In the 1930s, the Depression dominated the American scene. Labor unrest reached a peak, and there were many bloody skirmishes as workers struggled for the right to organize unions, engage in collective bargaining and call strikes. In Pennsylvania and other mining regions, company-paid "coal and iron police" crushed strikes by brute force. Elsewhere, injunctions were used to prevent workers from speaking out in public, going on strike or peacefully assembling.

During this period, the ACLU was caught up in the arduous task of defending the rights of labor. One of its biggest victories was against Mayor Frank Hague of Jersey City. Hague, whose motto was "I am the law," had continually prevented labor leaders from assembling or speaking in his city. The

ACLU, together with the Congress of Industrial Organizations, launched a court battle that finally did away with all bans on peaceful assembly anywhere in the United States.

The battle against censorship also got a big boost in this decade, with the ACLU winning a long legal fight to permit James Joyce's classic, *Ulysses,* to be circulated in the United States. The book had been kept out of the country because the government considered it "obscene."

The 1940s, on the whole, were not a bad time for civil liberties. Although America was caught up in the biggest war in its history, the people enjoyed far more personal freedom than they had during World War I and its aftermath. The ACLU also found that dissenters and conscientious objectors were treated much better than in the previous war.

However, one group of Americans—those of Japanese ancestry—were singled out for very harsh treatment. Fearing that the Japanese-Americans might aid the enemy in case of an attack on the West Coast, the government herded them into detention centers for the duration of the war. The ACLU objected loudly to this denial of freedom for people whose loyalty was never disproved, but its legal challenge and protests were useless.

In other areas, the ACLU was more effective. Under Union prodding, the Supreme Court finally ruled that Jehovah's Witnesses' children could not be expelled from school for refusing to salute the flag. The ACLU also succeeded in abolishing Texas' white primary; ending segregation in schools in Trenton, N. J.; and winning the franchise for Indians in Arizona and New Mexico.

During the 1950s, a "Cold War" chill settled on the nation. With the United States and the Soviet Union facing each other across a barrier of hostility, Americans became obsessed with the idea that communist "spies" and "traitors" were lurking in their midst. Fear was in the air, fanned by the loud and angry rhetoric of Senator Joseph McCarthy. Civil liberties faced possibly its gravest threat during this period, with McCarthy and his Senate investigating committee prying into the private lives of thousands of citizens in an effort to uncover communist links. He smeared reputations by innuendo rather than fact, and ruined countless careers. Just being called before McCarthy's committee was often enough to cause a man to lose his job. McCarthy searched for spies in the State Department and even in the Army, leading people to believe that spies were everywhere. He also attacked the ACLU as a "communist dominated" organization.

The ACLU fought hard against the repression of the '50s. It backed or led many court tests that eventually succeeded in curbing the worst abuses of investigating committees, abolishing loyalty oaths and creating an improved climate of respect for individual rights and freedoms.

In the field of black rights, the record of the 1950s was far brighter. The ACLU was one of many organizations that helped bring the case of *Brown vs. The Board of Education* to the Supreme Court in 1954. This case proved to be the first major breakthrough in the struggle to end segregation in the South. In it, the Court outlawed separate schools for whites and blacks, saying that "separate educational facilities are inherently unequal."

This case marked the start of a long series of court cases and legislation that, by the late 1960s, wiped out official segregation in public transportation, restaurants, hotels, theaters, private housing and elsewhere. The ACLU had a part in many of these civil rights victories, usually working side by side with other groups, such as the National Association for the Advancement of Colored People.

While this drive for equality was confined mainly to the courtroom in the 1950s, new tactics emerged in the turbulent 1960s. Young black students engaged in peaceful "sit-ins" in segregated southern restaurants, and whites and blacks together joined hands in "freedom rides" throughout the South. The ACLU supported these activities as new forms of the old idea of freedom of assembly and association.

Other groups, too, began to assert their rights of free speech and equality in the 1960s—students, women, homosexuals, prisoners, the poor and those regarded as mentally ill.

But the lingering, unpopular war in Vietnam came to overshadow all other issues by the late 1960s. It was the cause of student uprisings on campuses, mass demonstrations and a pervasive sense of unrest throughout the nation.

In an effort to gain national unity, the government began to clamp down on anti-war dissent. Pressure was put on news broadcasters to modify their reports. Students who engaged in anti-war protests were drafted earlier as a punishment. Vice President Spiro Agnew flayed the "radical-liberals" and young "punks" who were disrupting the country with their unpatriotic dissent. Attorney General John Mitchell was overheard to say cheerfully at a cocktail party, "This nation is going to go so far to the right that you won't recognize it."

Bracing itself for a new wave of political repression, the ACLU entered the 1970s with the same commitment to individual liberty that it had at its founding 50 years earlier. The Union was created to protect Americans from the intolerance and repression that had arisen from a world war—and 50 years later it was again defending personal freedom in a war-obsessed nation. But this was hardly surprising. As Roger Baldwin has often said, "No fight for civil liberties ever stays won."

This book is not a history of the American Civil Liberties Union. Rather, it is an attempt to show the many types of cases the ACLU feels are vital to the preservation of individual liberty in America. The focus is on the ACLU because it is the largest and most important organization of its type in America. For many years it was the *only* permanent civil liberties group serving all the people.

From an original membership of less than 50, the ACLU has grown over the last half century to an organization of more than 150,000 members in 1970. They belong to both the national group and a local affiliate. There are 48 affiliates throughout the United States, such as the New York Civil Liberties Union, the Massachusetts Civil Liberties Union, the Ohio Civil Liberties Union and so forth. They all cooperate with each other and follow a national policy line. Although there is general unity among them, there is not absolute uniformity. Policy is decided upon by a National Board of Directors, made up of 48 delegates who represent the affiliates, plus 30 at-large members. They meet every two months.

Most of the work of the ACLU and its affiliates goes on in the law courts. Over 1,000 lawyers throughout the country donate their services to the organization on a part-time basis, receiving no payment other than their expenses. They defend, free of charge, anyone the ACLU believes is a victim of injustice.

Most cases begin on the affiliate level, but the national ACLU will step in if help is needed or if a case has special significance. The national office has a full-time, paid legal staff that must approve the briefs of all ACLU cases that are taken to the

Supreme Court. Some of the affiliates have paid legal staffs of their own plus full-time directors, but other, smaller affiliates are run on a wholly voluntary basis.

Money comes from membership dues and private donations. Funds are distributed by the national office to the affiliates.

Not all of the ACLU's work is done in the courts. The organization also lobbies in Washington for or against bills affecting civil liberties; undertakes studies and educational projects; works with other organizations to further its aims; holds press conferences and sends out press releases and newsletters to publicize its activities; and engages in direct negotiations to try to settle conflicts out of court.

The ACLU's 150,000 members across the country serve as "watch-dogs" by reporting civil liberties violations whenever they occur. The membership includes businessmen, writers, teachers, lawyers, trade unionists, housewives, white-collar workers, clergymen, students, etc. They vary widely in age, occupation and political point of view, but are united in their concern for the Bill of Rights.

At the start of 1971, the ACLU and its affiliates were involved in thousands of cases, ranging over a very broad spectrum. Here is just a sampling of some of the routine, everyday ACLU cases:

- In Washington, the ACLU was defending a high school coed who was suspended from school for not wearing a brassiere under her clothing. The ACLU felt that as long as her manner of dress did not disrupt the classroom, she had the right to wear—or not wear—whatever she pleased;
- In Wisconsin, the ACLU was helping to appeal a six-month jail sentence that was imposed on the editor of

an underground newspaper. He had refused to tell a grand jury the name of the person who gave him some information about a bombing at the University of Wisconsin. Here, the ACLU was trying to protect "the public's right to the free flow of information," which would be threatened if reporters were forced to reveal their confidential sources;
- In Indiana, the ACLU was challenging a law that denied ex-convicts the right to become professional barbers. In New Jersey, the Union successfully fought a law denying some ex-convicts the right to vote;
- In Maryland, the ACLU helped a nudist win his legal fight to join the Baltimore police force. The man was fully qualified to become a policeman, but was denied a job because he spent his free time as a member of a nudist colony;
- In Virginia, the ACLU was challenging the practice of jailing alcoholics for public drunkenness, without providing treatment for the disease;
- In many states, the ACLU was battling laws that denied women the right to an abortion.

No case is too small for the ACLU to handle as long as the organization feels there is a denial of basic rights involved. Of course, not all people will agree with the Union's judgment in every case. Sometimes what the ACLU feels is an undue denial of freedom, others will feel is a necessary curbing of individual liberty for the benefit of society as a whole. At other times, people may feel the Union is not going far enough in its defense of individual freedom.

It is very hard to achieve a proper balance between personal liberty and the need for social order. No one can even say for sure what a "proper balance" is. But since the government is powerful while individuals are weak, it is very reassuring to know that there is a stable, non-partisan group that is always ready to stand up for the rights of the individual. The ACLU is there to see that people's rights and freedoms are not whittled away in the name of "law and order" or the "communist menace" or anything else.

As Alan Reitman, Associate Director of the ACLU, stated in a speech marking the organization's 50th anniversary:

"Our star remains the condition of human liberty, the protection and extension of that fragile but essential charter of freedom, the Bill of Rights."

[2]
WHEN JOHNNY REFUSES A GUN

"Hell, no! We won't go!"

This was the anti-war cry that reached an angry crescendo in the late 1960s, as thousands of young men protested against being drafted to fight in South Vietnam.

The resistance to the draft took many forms. At anti-war rallies and street demonstrations, young men openly burned their draft cards in defiance of the law. Others fled to Canada, or parts unknown, rather than serve in the armed forces. They remain there still—lonely exiles who face a jail sentence if they return to the United States.

In cafés and coffee houses where young people gather, posters are often tacked up on the walls telling them where they can get counseling on how to avoid the draft. Dr. Benjamin Spock, the famous baby doctor, was arrested and brought to trial with several other men who had been advising youngsters on ways to stay out of the army. They were all accused of obstructing the draft. Priests and nuns wound up in jail for their anti-war activities.

On the whole, this widespread reluctance to fight stemmed from the nature of the war in Vietnam. Many young people regarded it as an immoral and aggressive war. These same young men might have gone off willingly to fight against Hitler in World War II, but they would not fight in a war they considered unjust.

Only a small number of the anti-war protestors were actually pacifists or conscientious objectors—people who would not fight in *any* war because of deeply held religious or moral beliefs.

Such *absolute* pacifists have been part of the political scene in every American war, not just Vietnam. Their presence has posed some very difficult civil liberties problems. If a country is attacked or its freedom is threatened, the government has to call upon its citizens to fight. Sometimes a country can rely solely on a volunteer army, but more often it must draft men into battle or risk defeat.

Then some vital questions arise: Who should be drafted? Should all able-bodied men go off to fight or should some be exempt from the draft? In time of war, when men's very lives are at stake, isn't it highly unfair for some to be drafted and others spared?

On the other hand, how can a society that claims to respect individual rights force pacifists to bear arms if it is against their religious or moral beliefs? Is man's first duty to his conscience or his country? How do you tell if a man really has deep moral feelings against war or if he just wants to "cop out"? What if a war is aggressive rather than defensive, so that it is not a matter of survival at all? Should individuals be free to choose which wars they are willing to fight in? Could a country survive such freedom of choice if its security was at stake?

The American Civil Liberties Union has been grappling with questions like these for more than 50 years. In fact, the ACLU had its roots in the pacifist movement that sprang up before the outbreak of World War I. The Union's immediate predecessor, the National Civil Liberties Bureau, was set up in 1917 for the specific purpose of helping conscientious objectors during the war.

At that time, Congress did grant some exemptions from the draft, but only along very narrow religious lines. To qualify, a man had to be a member of "any *well-recognized* religious sect . . . whose . . . principles forbid its members to participate in war *in any form.*"

Jehovah's Witnesses, whose religion requires them to fight in the final battle of Armageddon but forbids fighting in any non-theistic conflict, did not qualify for exemptions under this law. When they refused to fight anyhow, they were sent to detention camps. So were members of other, more obscure religious sects that were not "well recognized." Practically the only ones who did qualify for religious exemptions were the Quakers and Mennonites.

Pacifists, socialists and others who would not fight for moral or political reasons were sent off to jail, where they served time alongside thieves, murderers and rapists.

The nation was so enraged at these conscientious objectors that it did not care how they were treated. In the jails and detention camps they were abused and harassed by the guards, and forced to do the most foul jobs. Although they were already paying for their anti-war beliefs by going to jail rather than serving in the army, they were still singled out for especially harsh treatment.

The National Civil Liberties Bureau tried to help these people as much as possible, but it accomplished little because of the nation's overwhelming hostility to pacifists.

After the war, when intolerance for personal freedom reached new heights, some leaders of the NCLB joined with other worried citizens to form the American Civil Liberties Union.

This was not a pacifist group, although it was deeply concerned about protecting the *rights* of pacifists, as well as the rights of all other political, social or religious dissenters.

The nation's contempt for pacifists continued well into the postwar years, when people turned their anger against aliens who held pacifist views. Many immigrants were seeking American citizenship at that time; but if they were suspected of being pacifists for either religious or moral reasons, their applications were turned down.

Aliens do not have an absolute *right* to become citizens; citizenship is a privilege granted to those who meet the country's requirements. In the 1920s, Congress required all applicants for citizenship to take an oath swearing to support and defend the Constitution and laws of the United States against all enemies, and to *bear arms* on behalf of the United States when required by law.

Many officials who were in charge of naturalization proceedings felt that Congress had meant to exclude pacifists by use of this oath. Although female pacifists would never be required by law to bear arms (at least not in pre-Women's Liberation days) they, too, were denied citizenship. The prejudice extended even to those who refused to kill because of religious beliefs.

A fairly typical case was that of Martha Graber, a member of the Mennonite religious sect. Miss Graber was born in Germany, but had been living with her parents in Lima, Ohio, since 1910. She took out her first citizenship papers in 1920, and applied for naturalization nine years later.

When it came time for her to take the citizenship oath, Miss Graber asked the judge if she could "affirm" rather than "swear." The judge, sensing a non-conformist in his midst, then asked each of the defendants before him if they would be willing to take a life in defense of this country.

When he came to Miss Graber, she said, "I conscientiously could not take life. I would be willing to do anything else, to give my own life for my country, but I could not take life."

The judge replied, "Well, I don't see why you want to become a citizen if you aren't willing to fight." Her application was denied.

Many other alien pacifists were also denied citizenship during this period, leading the American Civil Liberties Union to cry out against their exclusion. The organization felt that an individual's personal beliefs, whether religious, moral, philosophical or political, should have nothing to do with his eligibility for citizenship. Naturalized citizens should be entitled to the same freedom of thought and expression that native citizens enjoyed, the Union said. Otherwise, the country would be demanding more conformity of thought from naturalized citizens than from those who were born here.

The ACLU said that as long as a person promised to uphold the laws of the country, met the residency and language requirements and showed some understanding of the history and government of the United States, he should be able to become a citizen.

In asserting this position, the young ACLU took on its first case of major importance—that of Rosika Schwimmer.

Madame Schwimmer, a woman of international renown, was Hungarian by birth. She had served as a cabinet member in the moderate republican government of Hungary, which was ousted by a communist take-over in 1919. Although the communist regime was short-lived, Madame Schwimmer left the country and came to the United States as a resident alien. When she renounced her Hungarian citizenship, she became, in effect, a woman without a country.

She was widely known as a writer and lecturer, and had been

a leader of pacifist movements before and during World War I. Among her many activities, she had helped organize Henry Ford's Peace Ship Voyage to Europe, in a futile attempt to end the war.

She lectured everywhere, and was the first foreign woman ever to address the British Parliament. But when she tried to return to America after a trip abroad, an organization called the Woman Patriot Publishing Company asked FBI Director J. Edgar Hoover to bar her return. He declined to do so.

Shortly afterward, Madame Schwimmer applied for American citizenship. During her first hearing in a Chicago court, Federal Judge George A. Carpenter quizzed her at length about her willingness to bear arms in war. As a woman in her middle 50s, she would have been exempt from military service by both age and sex. Therefore, many of the judge's questions were purely hypothetical, resulting in a remarkable and absurd dialogue. Nevertheless, the judge's questions and statements offer a very accurate picture of how most Americans felt about pacifists at that time.

> Judge: . . . You say you are an uncompromising pacifist?
> Mme. Schwimmer: Yes.
> Judge: How far does that go? Does it refer only to yourself?
> Mme. Schwimmer: Yes.
> Judge: That you are not going to use your fists on somebody?
> Mme. Schwimmer: Yes.
> Judge: Or that you disapprove of the government fighting?
> Mme. Schwimmer: It means that I disapprove of the government asking me to fight.
> Judge: You mean fight personally?

Mme. Schwimmer: Yes, physically.

Judge: Carrying a gun?

Mme. Schwimmer: Yes.

Judge: Is that as far as it goes?

Mme. Schwimmer: That is as far as it goes.

Judge: . . . You do not care how many other women fight?

Mme. Schwimmer: I do not care because I consider it a question of conscience. If there are women fighters, it is their business.

Judge: Do you expect to spread this propaganda throughout the country with other women?

Mme. Schwimmer: Which propaganda, may I ask?

Judge: That you are an uncompromising pacifist and will not fight.

Mme. Schwimmer: Oh, of course. I am always ready to tell that to anyone who wants to hear it.

Judge: What is your occupation, Madame?

Mme. Schwimmer: I am a writer and lecturer.

Judge: And in your writing and in your lectures you take up the question of war and pacifism?

Mme. Schwimmer: If I am asked for that, I do.

Judge: . . . Now, I am not at all against people writing. There are a great many American citizens who are now decrying the possibility of the occurrence of war. They are against it. We have a great many pacifists in this country, but when the time comes and they are called out for their country, they forget all their views, all of the things they have been talking about, and start in on the defense of the home.

. . . If you were called to the service, and the kind of work that women usually can perform better than the men can—say as a nurse or as someone to give cheer to the soldiers—and you were at some place in a war, which I hope will never come, and you saw someone coming in the headquarters or the barracks, wherever it was, with a pistol in his hand to shoot the back of an officer of our country, and you had a pistol handy by, would you kill him?

Mme. Schwimmer: No, I would not.

Judge: The application is denied.

At this point, Madame Schwimmer's lawyers intervened and asked the judge to allow their client to explain herself more fully. One of the lawyers turned to her and said, "Under that same case, Mrs. Schwimmer, would you have given the officer any warning, if it was possible?"

Mme. Schwimmer: Certainly.

Lawyer: So that he could defend himself?

Mme. Schwimmer: Certainly. . . . I would try to hit the pistol out of the man's hand who tries to shoot. That is what I would try to do. . . .

Lawyer: Supposing that pistol had been pointed at you and you had a pistol?

Mme. Schwimmer: I would not defend myself. I mean I wouldn't take a pistol to defend myself even if you handed it to me, under no circumstances.

But Judge Carpenter insisted that if Madame Schwimmer would not be willing to kill the hypothetical assailant in this hypothetical case, she could not become a citizen. From his questions, it was clear that he objected to her writing and lecturing on pacifism, as well as her refusal to bear arms herself.

The American Civil Liberties Union offered to appeal Madame Schwimmer's case on the grounds that she was being denied citizenship because of her *views* rather than her conduct. The Union felt that as long as she was willing to comply with all laws that might possibly affect her, there were no valid grounds for not letting her become a citizen.

At first it seemed as if the ACLU's fight would be successful. A three-judge federal appeals court unanimously overturned Judge Carpenter's ruling, paving the way for Madame Schwimmer's naturalization. However, the federal government did not want such an outspoken pacifist to become a citizen, so it took the case to the Supreme Court.

On May 27, 1929, the Supreme Court handed down its decision in the *Schwimmer* case. The gist of it was that only people who were willing to kill for their country could become citizens of the United States.

The Court majority declared: "Whatever tends to lessen the willingness of citizens to discharge their duty to bear arms in the country's defense detracts from the strength and safety of the government . . . for if all or a large number of citizens oppose such defense, the 'good order and happiness' of the United States cannot long endure."

The majority's opinion provoked a ringing and eloquent dissent from Justice Oliver Wendell Holmes. In a now famous declaration, Justice Holmes called upon the nation to respect "the principle of free thought—not free thought for those who agree with us but freedom for the thought that we hate. I think we should adhere to that principle with regard to admission into, as well as life within, this country," he said.

Madame Schwimmer's pacifism was based on philosophical, not religious, beliefs. But Holmes pointed out that the Court's sweeping decision would also bar Quakers and other religious pacifists from citizenship.

"I would suggest that the Quakers have done their share to make the country what it is," he said. ". . . I had not supposed hitherto that we regretted our inability to expel them because they believe more than some of us do in the teachings of the Sermon on the Mount."

This was the first case that the ACLU had fought all the way up to the Supreme Court, and the negative decision came as a blow. Of all the rights and freedoms that the ACLU was trying to protect, perhaps the right *not* to kill was the most important to ACLU members, many of whom were pacifists themselves.

America continued to prevent alien pacifists from becoming citizens until 1946, when the Supreme Court finally reversed its decision in the *Schwimmer* case. Then the Court, in *Girouard vs. United States,* held that naturalization officials couldn't bar pacifists from citizenship unless Congress specifically said so.

But Congress never did. Instead, it ruled in 1952 that aliens who could not take an oath to bear arms because of "religious training and belief" might say instead that they would be willing to perform non-combatant service in the armed forces, or work of "national importance" under civilian direction. This opened the doors of citizenship to religious pacifists, although not to philosophical ones.

The new Supreme Court ruling, plus Congress' enactment, showed that the nation had mellowed in its attitude towards pacifists. As the patriotic ardor of the World War I era faded, the people's ability to tolerate these dissenters had broadened.

Some years prior to expanding the citizenship rights of pacifists, the government had also enlarged the grounds for pacifist draft exemptions. This was particularly remarkable in that the new ruling was passed in 1940, just when America was facing the threat of another, deadlier world war.

But times had changed, and the fanatical and buoyant patriotism of Americans during World War I—the war they thought would end all wars—had given way to a grim determination to fight again if necessary. Now Americans faced the menace of war with a soberness born from harsh experience, and they didn't indulge in the kind of excess patriotic zeal that had made life so miserable for dissenters during World War I.

With Hitler's armies swarming over Europe, America geared for the future by passing the first peacetime draft law in its history. Exemptions were granted to anyone who "by reason of religious training and belief is conscientiously opposed to participation in war in any form." Instead of bearing arms, these objectors could choose either non-combatant service or civilian work of national importance.

Pacifists no longer had to be members of "well-recognized" religious sects that specifically forbid their members to bear arms. However, they still had to be religious pacifists, rather than philosophical or political ones, even though the law was vague about requiring an absolute belief in God.

This still left many conscientious objectors who did not qualify for draft exemptions, including the Jehovah's Witnesses, who were disqualified because of their willingness to fight in Armageddon. When they, as well as non-religious pacifists, refused to serve in the armed forces, they were sent to jail.

However, the American Civil Liberties Union reported in 1942 that these objectors were being treated far better than in World War I. In jail, they were usually kept separate from the criminal prisoners, and received more humane treatment than before. Many were paroled to civilian service camps.

Although the ACLU has traditionally taken the position that drafting men into service is a violation of their basic rights and freedoms, it did not oppose the draft during World War II. This was the only time in its history that the Union chose not to oppose the draft. The reason for this lay in the winner-take-all nature of the war against fascism; if the democracies lost, *all* the rights and freedoms of the people would be destroyed. Thus, the urgent and compelling nature of this particular war led the majority of ACLU members to feel that it was better to give up some aspects of individual liberty temporarily in order to preserve a greater liberty in the future.

However, some ACLU members, including Roger Baldwin himself, kept up their private opposition to all forms of the draft, under *any* circumstances. They continued to feel that armies should be made up solely of men who had volunteered for battle, and that no person should have to make a choice between the Army or jail. These *absolute* civil libertarians formed only a small minority within the Union. But this did not mean that the Union as a whole would turn its back on conscientious objectors. During the war, the ACLU continued to watch out for their rights, and to press for an expansion of the grounds on which pacifists could be exempt from the draft.

After the war ended, eliminating the threat of fascism for the time being, the ACLU came out firmly against any peacetime continuation of the draft.

But within five years, armed conflict broke out in Korea. Although it was called a United Nations "peace action" rather than a war, America reactivated the draft. It has been with us ever since, in war and peace.

The Vietnam War has put the whole draft system under a severe strain. This is a war that is not really a "war" because Congress never declared it to be one. Also, it is a conflict that the American government cannot justify in lofty, moral terms. Our ally, the government of South Vietnam, is no more democratic than its communist enemy, the government of North Vietnam. Many Americans simply could not believe that we were there to protect the "freedom" of South Vietnam, but felt instead that our purpose was selfish. We wanted to secure American power and influence in Southeast Asia. Thus, we were interfering in what was basically a civil war to further our own aims, rather than securing freedom for anyone.

The top government leaders insisted that if South Vietnam fell to the communists, other Southeast Asian countries might topple like "dominoes." But people had grown tired of dire warnings about the communist menace, and couldn't believe that America's own security was at stake in far-off Vietnam.

Furthermore, we were inflicting great damage on the Vietnamese in the process of protecting them. Our soldiers defoliated their lands to flush out hidden guerrillas; burned hamlets that were suspected of being pro-Vietcong; and occasionally massacred Vietnamese civilians. To make matters worse, the Vietnamese people themselves didn't seem to care if they were taken over by the communists or not. They just wanted to be let alone.

Disillusionment over the war grew steadily, and by the late 1960s President Lyndon Johnson was utterly unable to convince the American people that they were fighting for a "just cause." The people distrusted Johnson's motives and disliked his policies so much that he did not try to run again for President in 1968.

Richard Nixon was elected President on a pledge to ease us

out of Vietnam and seek a "just and honorable peace." But to this date, he still has not been able to extricate the country from one of the most unpopular wars in its history.

Meanwhile, the draft goes on. A great many of those who are called to fight want no part of the war; they certainly don't want to risk dying in it while the President gropes for a face-saving way out.

Consequently, growing numbers of young men have turned to the Supreme Court, hoping that it would expand the grounds for draft exemptions by a broad reading of the Selective Service Act. The American Civil Liberties Union has been in the thick of this legal struggle, and has achieved a number of notable victories.

By 1970, the Supreme Court had come around to the view that young men could qualify as conscientious objectors for purely moral and ethical reasons. Their scruples against the war no longer had to stem from religious beliefs, the Court said, but they did have to be "deeply held."

Under this ruling, the Court exempted from military service "all those whose consciences, spurred by deeply held moral, ethical or religious beliefs, would give them no rest or peace if they allowed themselves to become part of an instrument of war."

But this meant *all* war, so the ruling was no help to those who opposed only the Vietnam War.

The crucial question that the ACLU tried to bring to the Supreme Court was whether young men could qualify as conscientious objectors if they were opposed to *some* wars but not to all wars.

To test the doctrine of selective conscientious objection, the ACLU took on the case of Air Force Captain Dale Noyd. Captain Noyd, a veteran of 12 years in the Air Force and winner of the Air Force Commendation Medal, had shocked his colleagues in December 1966 by applying for resignation from the Air Force as a conscientious objector. If he could not be released, he said, he wished at least to be reassigned to duties that would not conflict with his beliefs. At the time, Captain Noyd was an assistant professor of psychology and leadership at the Air Force Academy in Colorado Springs. However, he knew that he was about to be sent to an Air Force training unit in New Mexico, where he would have to train young pilots as replacements for the Vietnam War. This, he felt, would be against his conscience.

While serving in the Air Force, Captain Noyd had developed deep moral feelings about war, mankind and life itself, which he called "humanism." These views stemmed from his readings and studies, and led him to feel intensely that he must "never be used as an instrument of aggression," although he would support the use of force for defense. The Vietnam War, he felt, was "unjust and immoral." Thus, he could not participate in it directly, through a combat assignment, or even indirectly through a combat-support job.

In January 1967, Captain Noyd was told that his request for conscientious objector status had been turned down because the authorities did not believe he qualified. In addition, he was not allowed to resign because it "would not be in the best interest of the Air Force."

Instead, Captain Noyd received orders to report on April 1 to the 27th Tactical Fighter Wing, Cannon Air Force Base, New Mexico.

At this point, the American Civil Liberties Union stepped into the case and tried to get the courts to stop the Air Force from sending Captain Noyd to New Mexico. When this legal maneuver failed, Captain Noyd reported to Cannon Air Force

Base as ordered. Once there, he refused to obey orders to train pilots for service in Vietnam. The Air Force accused him of "willful disobedience," and brought him up on court-martial charges.

While awaiting trial, Captain Noyd wrote a letter to the Washington affiliate of the ACLU. He had been working very closely with the Union during his difficult legal struggle, and had developed such admiration for it that he applied for a job with the Washington branch. However, his letter reveals his pessimism about the outcome of his case, and his certainty that he would have to go to jail because of his views. He says, "I must confess that had it not been for my present predicament and my frequent association with the ACLU people over the past 14 months, I would not now be considering any position other than on a university faculty. . . . If nothing else, my personal involvement with such an issue and with ACLU have instituted a lifetime of social activism and respect and affection for the work—and people—of ACLU. . . .

"No matter how competent and thorough my defense at the court-martial, I shall certainly be adjudged 'guilty,' with the absolute minimum sentence of dismissal from the service. I personally expect a period of confinement—although of what duration I can't begin to guess. We shall appeal through the civil courts on the 'selective c.o.' issue, but Marvin [Karpatkin] and Jack [Pemberton] have warned me that even in the Supreme Court the prognosis is not good." (Mr. Karpatkin was the ACLU lawyer who defended Captain Noyd, and Mr. Pemberton was at that time ACLU Executive Director.)

The letter is a good illustration of the fact that many, many times the ACLU goes to court on behalf of cases it knows it can't win. But in each case, the Union is probing and testing, hoping to find chinks in unjust laws or trying to push the courts into new interpretations of old laws. Just the fact that cases are heard in open court makes the public more aware of the issues involved and helps build up pressure for change.

Captain Noyd was right about his own court-martial. He was convicted and sentenced to one year at hard labor, a bad conduct discharge and forfeiture of all pay and allowances.

The ACLU appealed the decision immediately, and was able to prevent the Air Force from sending Captain Noyd to the Disciplinary Barracks at Fort Leavenworth, Kansas, while the appeals were pending. However, he was held in detention at Clovis Air Force Base in New Mexico during the whole legal process. By the time the ACLU had pushed his case up to the highest tribunals, Captain Noyd had already served his full year term. Thus, the Supreme Court and the U. S. Court of Military Appeals refused to hear the case.

This was a dreary anti-climax for such an important case. It was the first time that the question of conscientious objection to a particular war had been brought to court, and it would have opened up the whole issue of whether men might be allowed to distinguish between "just wars" and "unjust wars."

The ACLU feels very strongly that men who are not strict pacifists, "but object only to what they believe is an unjust war, should not be forced to participate in a particular war if their objection comes from the same depth of conscience." This belief is shared by the World Council of Churches, the Lutheran Church in America, the Conference of Catholic Bishops and the American Jewish Congress.

However, the federal government feels that leaving men free to serve only in wars they personally consider "just" would seriously weaken the nation's fighting strength. In addition, the Nixon administration has argued that no matter how sincere or religious *selective* conscientious objectors might be, a political judgment lies at the heart of their objection, and this cannot be considered valid grounds for a draft exemption. In an effort to protect the nation's security, the Nixon administration has strongly opposed the idea of selective conscientious objection.

Nevertheless, the legal fight that the ACLU started was taken up by others, and it was not long after Captain Noyd's case ended that another case of selective conscientious objection loomed before the Supreme Court. On March 8, 1971, the Court handed down a negative ruling in this case, saying that only men who opposed *all* wars could qualify for draft exemptions. This was justified, the Court said, by "the government's interest in procuring the manpower necessary for military purposes." However, the lone dissenter in the 8–1 decision, Justice William O. Douglas, declared: "I had assumed that the welfare of the single human soul was the ultimate test of the vitality of the First Amendment."

The draft laws have been the cause of many civil liberties complaints. One of the most serious charges during the Vietnam War was that the draft laws were being used to punish anti-war dissenters.

In October 1967, the Director of the Selective Service, Lieutenant General Lewis B. Hershey, sent a letter to all draft boards saying that anyone who violated the draft laws "or the related processes" should be denied deferment "in the national interest."

In practice, this meant that young men who joined in anti-war protests would be stripped of their deferments, reclassified 1–A and drafted as punishment for their actions.

The American Civil Liberties Union was outraged by this misuse of the draft laws to suppress dissent, and rapidly filed six lawsuits aimed at halting the practice. The suits involved students, ministers and one young man who had been draft-exempt for health reasons. Each of these men saw their draft status changed to 1–A by their local boards because they had protested against American policy in Vietnam.

The ACLU felt that the local draft boards had no power to do this because even if the men had violated some laws, they could not be judged guilty and punished without a trial. That was a denial of due process of law. As a blatant example of draft abuse, the ACLU cited the case of John Ratliff, a student at the University of Oklahoma who lost his student deferment because his local draft board felt that his active membership in the Students for a Democratic Society was not "in the best interests of the government."

The first of the ACLU test cases to reach the Supreme Court was *Oestereich vs. Selective Service Board No. 11*. James Oestereich, a student at Andover Theological Seminary in Boston, had held a 4–D (ministerial student) draft exemption.

On October 20, 1967, he and 356 other young dissenters had sent draft cards back to the Department of Justice in a protest against the Vietnam War. They did this, they wrote, as "an act of collective conscience in support of our dying and suffering brothers who are presently fighting on our behalf in Vietnam." They said they did not believe the Vietnam War was a "just war," but rather that it was "a major threat to the security and peace of the world."

On November 7, Oestereich received a letter telling him he had been reclassified to 1–A status, and was ordered to report at once for induction into the Army.

The ACLU was able to delay his induction while it filed an appeal, and one year later the Supreme Court handed down its decision in the *Oestereich* case. Speaking for the majority, Justice William O. Douglas made it very clear that when

Congress grants exemptions to the draft law, and a man meets all the terms and conditions for an exemption, local draft boards cannot take it away because of actions not related to the reasons for the exemption.

If they could, Douglas said, it "would make the draft boards free-wheeling agencies meting out their brand of justice in a vindictive manner . . . We deal with conduct of a local Board that is basically lawless."

If such behavior was allowed, Douglas went on, it would mean that local boards could induct a minister or anyone else simply to get even with him for his political, religious or racial views, or even "to get him out of town so that the amorous interests of a Board member might be better served." He concluded that the local draft board had clearly exceeded its powers.

The ACLU's victory in the *Oestereich* case was followed by successes in other, similar "punitive draft" cases. All were part of a well-coordinated legal attack by the ACLU that challenged the arbitrary use of power by the Selective Service System.

The ACLU felt that General Hershey had lauched his punitive draft policy "in notorious disregard of First Amendment guarantees of freedom of speech and assembly," and in violation of the Selective Service Act passed by Congress.

Applauding the Supreme Court decisions in these cases, the ACLU said they called a halt "to the use of the draft as an instrument of official retaliation against those who disagree with government policy."

Although the ACLU has traditionally opposed the idea of drafting men for combat, it has never encouraged defiance of the draft laws. Instead it has worked for their repeal. In May 1969, the Union came out with its strongest statement urging the end of the draft. It declared:

> Military conscription is a severe infringement of individual liberties, at best the resort of a nation facing an imminent threat. It must rest upon the interests of national security, what James Madison called 'the impulse of self-preservation.' ACLU believes that government has the duty to prove to the public that so drastic a step as conscription is required today. No such showing has been made. Instead, conscription has become a habit of mind for the nation, winning a lazy acceptance from adults beyond its reach, but creating havoc and hostility from young men whose lives it disrupts and too often takes. It is shameful for a free nation to continue for 30 years a form of involuntary servitude without regular and conclusive showings of its necessity.

While the Union does not rule out the use of a draft in times of genuine danger to the country, it does not believe that this is such a time. Certainly, the government hasn't proved satisfactorily that America's freedom or security is at stake in Vietnam. Thus, the ACLU feels, there is no valid reason at present for the government to curtail men's liberties by drafting them into service.

Just as the war created acute dissension throughout the country, it also caused strife within the ACLU. During the early days of the anti-Vietnam War demonstrations, the Union was split over whether or not to defend draft resisters—men who refused to serve or obstructed the draft for mainly political reasons, and could not be defended as conscientious objectors.

These young men were openly defying the government because they felt the Vietnam War was both unconstitutional and unjust. They were engaging in civil disobedience. The ACLU has taken on civil disobedience cases only when it felt the law in question was *unconstitutional,* and the defiance of it was non-violent (such as the peaceful sit-ins by black students in the South to protest the segregation laws).

But now the ACLU began to divide along "traditional" and "expansionist" lines involving questions of what was constitutional and what was not, and which direction the Union should take. The "traditionalists" wanted the ACLU to stay within its historical boundaries, concentrating on issues that involved clear-cut violations of civil liberties. They did not want to defend men who refused to register for the draft, because they felt that conscription in general was not unconstitutional, even though the current draft law was a "violation of civil liberties."

The "expansionists," on the other hand, interpreted civil liberties in a much broader way, and refused to place traditional limits on the types of cases the ACLU could handle. The "expansionists" considered the draft unconstitutional, and were willing to defend anyone who defied it. Most important, the "expansionists" wanted the ACLU to take a public stand against the war itself—something the Union had never done in any previous war because such an action was thought to lie outside the sphere of civil liberties.

For a while, the "traditionalists" were in the majority, but as the war dragged on, some of the strongest affiliates, such as those in New York, New Jersey and Massachusetts, worked to sway the others to their own expansionist point of view. In some instances, these affiliates publicly took positions on war-related issues different from those of the national office.

In June 1970, the ACLU formally announced its opposition

to the Vietnam War, stating that the conflict had a "highly detrimental effect on civil liberties."

This was a major departure from the organization's traditional role as a defender of individual rights, but ACLU Executive Director John de J. Pemberton insisted that the Union was still a non-partisan organization despite its anti-war position. "We have never before identified war itself as the cause of civil liberties deprivation," he said in explaining the change in ACLU policy.

The Union charged that the war "fostered an atmosphere of violence which has resulted in the slaying of college students and black people, violent attacks on and by demonstrators both for and against the war, and a climate of repression in which attempts have been made to stifle criticism of the war."

Among the things that the war was responsible for, the ACLU said, was:

- Continuation of the draft;
- Stifling of dissent by the government;
- Intense anger and frustration on the part of students that prompted them to use terror tactics, such as burning buildings, destroying files and holding hostages;
- Government repression of these students, creating an atmosphere in which academic freedom became impossible;
- Urban neglect because of the need to divert resources to the war effort;
- Attempts by the government to curb freedom of the press, especially when the newspapers and television showed a growing dislike for the war;
- An increase in military domination of policy.

All these factors, plus the American people's alarming trend towards dissent by violence, rather than by peaceful action or dialogue, led the ACLU to feel that the situation was urgent. "Therefore," the Union declared, "to preserve civil liberties, which provide the mechanism for peaceful change, the American Civil Liberties Union insists that the war in Southeast Asia must stop."

The ACLU also stated that the Vietnam War was unconstitutional because only Congress had the power to declare war, and it had never done so in Vietnam.

Because of this, the ACLU said it would work to defend a law passed by the state of Massachusetts declaring that no citizen of that state could be sent abroad to fight without a Congressional declaration of war. Massachusetts was trying to bring this issue before the Supreme Court to get a final ruling on the war's legality. However, the Court declined to hear the case.

The war still drags on. It has caused momentous upheavals within our society, and the ACLU feels that it has already made deep inroads on the Bill of Rights, and that the longer it lasts, the greater the danger will be to personal rights and freedoms.

[3]
FLAGS AND FANATICS

One night in April 1970, the Yippie leader Abbie Hoffman was appearing on a television talk show. After he had been on camera a few minutes, he removed the jacket he was wearing. At that point, the television station blacked him off the screen. For the rest of the show, viewers could hear Mr. Hoffman's disembodied voice, but they could not see him.

The reason for the blackout was that under his jacket, Mr. Hoffman was wearing a shirt made out of an American flag. The TV station, fearing that legal difficulties might arise from Mr. Hoffman's mockery of the flag, avoided trouble by not showing him.

The American flag itself became a symbol of controversy during the nationwide unrest of the 1960s and early 1970s. Many Americans started using flag decals on their automobiles to symbolize their support for "law and order," and their general approval of the American position in Vietnam. Others retaliated by using flag decals with peace symbols on them to stress that although they were loyal Americans, they did not support the war. Still others displayed flag decals superimposed over black hands to emphasize their support of the black revolution. Radicals like Mr. Hoffman tried to show their contempt for the "establishment" by tearing up the flag in public or burning it.

These varied uses and abuses of the American flag have revived an old legal question: to what extent must people publicly honor a *symbol* or, conversely, to what extent must they not dishonor it?

Every state in the union has laws against desecration of the flag. "Desecration" is a rather vague term, but in general it means showing contempt for or hurling abuse at something sacred. The American Civil Liberties Union believes that all laws making it a crime to "desecrate" the American flag are *unconstitutional*. Actions against the flag harm no one. They are just symbolic substitutes for speech—and as such they are protected by the First Amendment guarantees of freedom of speech, the ACLU feels.

Since the 1960s, the ACLU has been swamped with flag desecration cases. *Civil Liberties,* the ACLU's monthly publication, reported 19 flag cases pending in September 1970.

Although the number of such cases had risen to new heights, they were hardly a new phenomenon. The ACLU has been battling flag laws since the 1920s. A glance at the ACLU files is all that it takes to see that the American flag has aroused heated, often hysterical emotions in people over the years, and that great injustices have been done in the name of "patriotism."

One of the saddest cases on record occurred in June 1927. A small item in the ACLU files revealed that nine-year-old Russell Tremain, son of Mr. and Mrs. J. W. Tremain of Bellingham, Wash., had been brought to court by school officials because of his parents' refusal to let him salute the flag. The Tremains belonged to a religious sect that forbade saluting as sacrilegious.

Because of this so-called crime, Judge W. P. Brown "permanently" removed Russell from the custody of his parents and put him up for adoption with "Christian, patriotic parents."

The Tremains could not fight this action legally since their

Flags and Fanatics [53]

religion did not recognize "earthly courts." Thus, there was nothing the ACLU could do for them except publicize the case. Russell was sent to the County Detention Home, where he was placed on a list of those eligible for adoption.

Six months later, however, a Superior Court judge ordered Russell Tremain returned to his parents after they said they would give him a "proper education."

The 1920s and 1930s were years of harsh intolerance for those who refused to honor the patriotic symbols. When Joseph Flane forgot to remove his hat during a salute to the flag at the New York City parade for aviator Charles A. Lindbergh, a policeman pulled him out of the crowd and arrested him. Mr. Flane spent two days in jail.

This incident outraged the ACLU, which sent the following letter of protest to the *New York Evening Telegram:* "Love of country and reverence for the flag are sentiments which cannot be dictated according to code and ceremonials. They are matters of personal feeling. Police clubs and magistrates courts cannot inspire them. A nation and a flag that are worthy of reverence will inspire it by their dignity and worth in relation to the lives of citizens."

One of the most outrageous flag cases of this period involved a communist children's camp in upper New York state. The camp was not flying any flag at all, a fact that enraged members of the Ku Klux Klan who lived just across the state line in Pennsylvania.

One evening, the Klan members donned their white sheets, crossed over into New York and surrounded the camp. They had brought an American flag with them, and tried to force the camp directors to put it up. The directors refused. In an attempt to intimidate them, the KKK put up a huge cross near the camp and set it on fire.

Finally, the state police came—and arrested the camp directors for refusing to fly the flag. At the station house, the directors were forced to kiss the flag. Later, they were sentenced to three months in jail for "desecrating the American flag."

The American Civil Liberties Union filed an appeal, stating that the camp directors' conviction was "absurd, even for a communist case. The young women did not desecrate the flag. They simply refused to accept an American flag from members of the KKK who insisted that the camp display that symbol of patriotism."

In those years, the ACLU handled many flag cases of this type, but legal victories were rare. It wasn't until the Jehovah's Witnesses cases of the 1940s that the ACLU made its first major breakthrough against the flag salute laws.

The Jehovah's Witnesses were a small, aggressive religious sect whose beliefs clashed with many of the accepted values of American society. The Witnesses would not fight in any war; they would not participate in political affairs; and they forbade the worship of images, which meant to them that they could not salute the flag.

They were a very unpopular group, but not for their religious views alone. Each Witness was supposed to go out and actively recruit new members for the sect, so that sometimes whole groups of them would enter a town to preach on street corners, distribute literature, solicit funds or push their way into people's homes to play their religious records. They themselves were not very tolerant of other religions, so that their behavior was sure to antagonize people.

In small towns, especially, the Witnesses were heartily disliked. Local officials would use any ordinance they could find as an excuse to put them in jail or harass them. They were jailed for disturbing the peace, soliciting funds without a permit, parading without a license, etc.

But the Witnesses made good use of the legal system, appealing many of their convictions on the grounds of religious freedom. Between 1938 and 1943, 16 major cases involving the Jehovah's Witnesses reached the Supreme Court. Among them were the flag salute cases, in which the American Civil Liberties Union defended the Witnesses' right to refuse to salute the flag on religious grounds.

The Witnesses had suffered a great deal because of their refusal to salute. In many states, their children were expelled from the public schools because they would not participate in the flag exercises. For example, in Denver, Colorado, 50 Jehovah's Witnesses' children were expelled in one year.

The ACLU wanted a Supreme Court ruling on the issue, hoping for a favorable verdict that would guarantee the Witnesses' children their right to a public school education in any state in the nation, regardless of whether or not they would salute the flag.

In 1940, one flag salute case finally reached the Supreme Court. It centered around two Jehovah's Witnesses' youngsters who had been expelled from a public school for failing to salute. The basic question in the case was whether saluting the flag was so vital in building patriotism that it outweighed any religious taboos against saluting.

Much to the ACLU's disappointment, the Supreme Court ruled, in effect, that it was up to each state to decide the matter for itself. The Court felt it could not interfere with flag-saluting rules if a state regarded them as important in fostering national unity.

But shortly afterwards, the Supreme Court did a surprising

about-face. Three of the justices who had voted against the Witnesses announced that they now felt they had been wrong. By 1943, the Supreme Court took on another flag salute case so that it could reconsider the problem.

In this case, the Supreme Court reversed its decision of just three years earlier. The Court now ruled that the First Amendment freedoms, including freedom of religion, held a "preferred position" in American society, and could not be suppressed unless they created a "clear and present danger." Since failure to salute the flag for religious reasons did not create this kind of danger, the laws requiring it were unconstitutional. People could not be forced to join in a purely symbolic ceremony such as flag saluting, the Court said.

This was a great victory for the American Civil Liberties Union, which had been fighting flag salute laws for more than 20 years. The ACLU had come out against these laws at a time when the vast majority of Americans firmly supported them, as did the courts. The ACLU's unpopular position only added to its reputation as an "unpatriotic" group. Nevertheless, it kept pressing the fight until it won.

Today, people are no longer put in jail for refusing to salute the flag, failing to remove their hat before it or refusing to pay it homage in any other way. This type of action is no longer thought of as "desecration," in a legal sense.

The flag cases that arose during the 1960s were quite different. In the earlier years, people were punished mainly for *ignoring* the flag, for refusing to make patriotic gestures towards it; in short, for refusing to conform to accepted notions of patriotism. But in recent years, people have been tampering with the flag, rather than just ignoring it. They have altered its appearance with various peace symbols, flown it upside down, made shirts out of it or mutilated it.

Such acts have brought them face to face with the flag desecration laws that exist in every state, for these laws make it a crime to abuse the flag. Thus, while people are no longer forced to salute the flag or honor it in public, there are still laws to prevent them from physically dishonoring it.

The ACLU has been trying to get the courts to declare these laws unconstitutional on the grounds that they interfere with the freedom of expression guaranteed by the First Amendment, but it has not been successful so far. At most, the courts have only ruled that some desecration laws were too "vague," or that a particular action did not fall within the scope of the law.

Among the flag desecration cases fought by the American Civil Liberties Union in recent years was one involving Mrs. Betsy Hubner, a housewife from Long Island, N. Y. In November 1969, Mrs. Hubner flew the American flag upside down as a protest against the war in Vietnam. Traditionally, an upside-down flag is a distress signal.

Her action was part of a nationwide anti-war moratorium that had been planned for that day. An unidentified neighbor complained to the police, who promptly showed up at Mrs. Hubner's house. They demanded that she remove the flag immediately, or turn it right side up. Mrs. Hubner refused and was handed a summons that charged her with violating part of the state's General Business Law, which prohibited showing contempt "either by word or act" for the flag.

When Mrs. Hubner appeared in court the following month, Judge James Griffin set her bail at $500—a high amount for this type of offense. To make matters worse, the bail bondsman was so overwhelmed by patriotic ardor that he refused to provide bond for her "as a matter of principle."

Mrs. Hubner was then searched, handcuffed, fingerprinted

and put in jail until her husband was able to get $500 to bail her out.

When the case came to trial, the New York Civil Liberties Union defended Mrs. Hubner on the grounds that her act was symbolic speech, protected by the First Amendment.

Mrs. Hubner won her case. In a strongly worded opinion, the judge agreed that she had not defiled the flag. "It is very difficult for me to see that an act of turning a flag upside down . . . in any way indicates a dishonorment or defiling of the flag. Certainly the act would be an opinion on the part of the person that she and the country was in distress."

In this case, as in others, the court did not rule on the constitutionality of New York's flag desecration law; it said only that flying the flag upside down was not an act of desecration.

The ACLU is quick to point out that when the American flag is used for non-political purposes—even crude and tasteless ones—no one is sent to jail for it. For example, the American flag design has been used on toilet lids, dinnerware, piggy banks and beer serving trays. It has also been fashioned into bikinis, curtains, ties and vests. When Roy Rogers and Dale Evans wore American flag vests years ago as a patriotic gesture, they were not accused of flag desecration. But when Abbie Hoffman wore a flag shirt, he was not permitted to be televised. From this it would seem that only political dissenters are being charged with flag desecration, while non-political people are free to use the flag however they please.

In 1967, the Union brought another flag case all the way up to the Supreme Court, but won only a partial victory. The case involved a World War II Bronze Star veteran who had burned an American flag as a protest gesture. In June 1966, black veteran Sidney Street was at home in Brooklyn listening to his

Flags and Fanatics [59]

radio when he heard a news bulletin that civil rights leader James Meredith had been shot during his Mississippi march. Mr. Street felt that the government had failed to protect Meredith, and was so enraged that he took an old 48-star American flag from his drawer, ran out into the street and set fire to the flag.

About 30 people clustered around Mr. Street, who told them, "We don't need no damn flag." When the police came and asked Mr. Street if he was the one who had burned the flag, he said: "Yes, that is my flag; I burned it. If they let that happen to Meredith, we don't need an American flag."

Mr. Street was tried and convicted for desecrating the American flag. The ACLU hoped the Supreme Court would overturn Mr. Street's conviction on the grounds that the flag desecration law was unconstitutional, and that burning a flag was not a criminal offense.

The Supreme Court did overturn Mr. Street's conviction, but for entirely different reasons. The justices felt that his conviction may have been based partly on what he *said* about the flag, rather than what he did to it. This, the justices felt, would be wrong.

Although the ACLU lost many flag cases in the 1960s, it began winning more by the end of the decade as the courts began to unbend. In 1970, *Civil Liberties,* the ACLU publication, reported the following victories around the country:

- In Minnesota, a man was acquitted of flag desecration for displaying an American flag that had a peace symbol instead of stars. The court ruled that because of the different design, the flag was not an American flag within the meaning of the law;
- In Colorado, a student who dramatically ripped a flag as

part of a classroom speech was reinstated in school by a court order. He had been expelled under a state law banning behavior "inimical to the welfare, safety and morals of other pupils";
- In Washington, a man was acquitted of desecration charges for sewing a flag to the roof of his car;
- In a Pennsylvania case, a student was acquitted after having worn the flag as a kerchief to symbolize that she was in mourning for the war dead;
- Another Pennsylvania student was acquitted for carrying an American flag at a parade that had on it the words "Make love not war" and "the new American revolutionaries."

Among the many cases pending at the end of 1970 was one involving an Illinois professor who was due to be tried for decorating his car with a flag decal that had a peace symbol on it. If convicted, he could be sentenced to five years in jail and a $5,000 fine. The most alarming aspect of this case is that under Illinois law, half the fine would go to the local school board and half to the person who filed the complaint against him. In this case, the complainant was a vigilante group. Under such a law, it can become very profitable for citizens to turn each other in on flag desecration charges.

How might an ordinary flag desecration case (or any case) come to the attention of the ACLU? A fairly typical example was the case of David Fitch, a young man who owned a psychedelic poster shop in Las Vegas, Nevada.

In 1968, the Las Vegas police filed flag desecration charges against Mr. Fitch for displaying a poster of an American

Flags and Fanatics [61]

flag with daisies in the upper left-hand corner, where the stars should have been.

It was the first case of this type in the state of Nevada, so it attracted some attention. Mr. Fitch's lawyer argued that the object in question was not an actual flag but a poster, so that it was not a matter of flag desecration at all.

However, the judge said that any reasonable man would have no doubt that the poster was a representation of the flag. The verdict was "guilty."

Afterwards, Mr. Fitch sent a letter to Lawrence Speiser, director of the Washington office of the ACLU. Mr. Speiser, in turn, sent the letter on to Melvin Wulf, Legal Director of the ACLU in New York, who is mainly responsible for deciding which cases the ACLU will take to the Supreme Court.

Mr. Fitch's letter was as follows:

4/16/68

Dear Mr. Speiser,

I spoke to you briefly about this case when you were in Las Vegas earlier this year. I was fined $500 last week in Municipal Court. The case comes up in District Court this May. There is a strong chance I will lose there as well. My attorney, Dean Breeze, . . . is not going to charge me any more for the District Court representation. I understand there are some good precedents in my favor. I cannot afford to take it to the Supreme Court. Bob Throckmorton of the local ACLU told me that you might be the one to ask about having the ACLU appeal the case to the U. S. Supreme Court. The manufacturer has written me a letter stating that 7,200 flag posters have been sold across the U. S. with no other criticisms, much less arrests. He states the reason he made the poster was to symbolize youth and national spirit.

I have never been arrested before, and the whole episode has been traumatic. With your help I hope we can get this law off the books so no one else has to go through a similar ordeal. I hope to hear from you at your earliest convenience.

Sincerely,
David Fitch

A few weeks later, Mr. Fitch received the following reply from the ACLU in New York:

May 9, 1968

Dear Mr. Fitch,

Larry Speiser has forwarded your April 16 letter to me.

We will of course be agreeable to representing you on appeal to the U. S. Supreme Court. I take it from your letter that there is still an appeal available to you to the Nevada Supreme Court. Who is representing you in that appeal? That, too, should be an ACLU case.

Why don't you call me collect when you receive this letter so that we can discuss it.

Sincerely yours,
Melvin L. Wulf
Legal Director

With so many flag desecration cases on the dockets, the Supreme Court is bound to hand down more conclusive rulings on the subject eventually. Meanwhile, the ACLU is taking on all the cases of this type it can find in an effort to have all flag desecration laws wiped off the books.

[4]
WHITE LIBERALS AND BLACK MEN

In the closing scenes of the 1915 Civil War movie spectacular *Birth of a Nation,* bands of lawless black men are shown vandalizing, looting and burning southern towns and raping white women. Just at the point where the movie's white heroine is about to be attacked by black men, she is rescued by her saviors —the Ku Klux Klan. Throughout the South, the Klansmen and the blacks engage in fierce battles and, in the end, the Klan triumphantly restores white power to the South.

Birth of a Nation became a classic of the movie industry. It was the first "spectacular" that told more than just a simple story, and it employed many new movie-making techniques. However, the film was also guilty of glorifying the Ku Klux Klan and depicting blacks as lawless animals.

For many years, the National Association for the Advancement of Colored People tried to prevent the showing of *Birth of a Nation,* charging that the film aroused white audiences to fury and fanned race hatred against a minority that couldn't defend itself. But the American Civil Liberties Union opposed the NAACP's efforts to ban the film, taking the position that there must be no curbs on free speech, however obnoxious that speech may be.

This clash stemmed from the different natures of the two civil rights groups. The NAACP's vital concern was to gain equal rights and freedoms for *blacks;* everything else was secondary. But the ACLU's purpose was to protect the basic rights of *all* Americans, rather than those of any one group. Sometimes these goals conflicted.

The ACLU is made up mainly of white, middle-class Americans who have far-ranging concerns about civil rights and freedoms in America. Their concern includes equal rights for blacks and other minority groups, but it is not limited to that. The ACLU regards the NAACP, the Congress of Racial Equality and other black civil rights groups as the primary organizations in the battle to end racial discrimination. The ACLU assists them in this fight whenever it can, and frequently takes on race cases on its own, but still sees itself as a secondary force in this area.

However, as black-white tensions polarized the nation to a frightening degree in the 1960s, and both sides reacted with violence, the ACLU stepped up its activities on behalf of black peoples' rights. This was done out of a sense of urgency, for it had become obvious that if America did not solve its racial problems in a fair and just manner, the counter-forces of black militancy and white repression would spiral out of control.

The ACLU's deep involvement in the race issue was a dramatic change from its policy of 50 years ago, when it would not intervene in black matters. Partly because of the clash over *Birth of a Nation,* the ACLU and the NAACP worked in separate spheres, by mutual agreement. The NAACP handled all cases involving black rights by itself; the ACLU concentrated on cases dealing with whites. The only racial minorities the ACLU concerned itself with were Indians and Orientals. Even in lynching cases, the ACLU became involved only if the victim was white.

However, by 1930, a number of southern states began updating old anti-Negro laws to prevent blacks from forming their own labor unions or getting into all-white unions. The ACLU, which was deeply caught up in the struggle for the rights of labor, started taking an interest in the black worker as well as the white one.

At that time, the outlook for gaining any rights for southern blacks was very bleak. They were kept "in their place" by terror tactics (25 lynchings between 1925 and 1930), and by state laws that were strictly enforced. Segregation was legally required by 17 states. In 30 states, racial intermarriage was forbidden. Mississippi even had a law that made it a crime to *advocate* the social equality of the races.

In 1931, the ACLU issued its first pamphlet on the racial situation in America, *Black Justice*. This was a survey of the many injustices that were being done to blacks in both the North and the South: denial of voting rights; racial slums and ghettos; exclusion of blacks from juries; job discrimination; and widespread segregation in every phase of public and private life. In addition, many southern states had laws that prevented blacks from leaving because southern whites wanted them around as a cheap labor force.

The pamphlet did not do much to stir up America's indignation, but it did result in the resignation of a few southern ACLU members who did not like the new direction the Union was taking.

In its annual report for 1933–34, the Union criticized the American Federation of Labor because so many of its unions barred blacks. It also attacked the National Recovery Administration's policy of paying southern blacks less than southern whites for the same type of work.

With the advent of the Scottsboro boys' trial in the mid-1930s, the ACLU became more actively involved in matters of racial discrimination. The case revolved around nine black boys in Scottsboro, Alabama, who were accused of raping two white girls while all eleven of them were hitching a ride on a freight train. Although it was pretty clear that the girls were prostitutes and had not been forced to do anything they didn't want to do, the boys were convicted anyhow. Under Alabama law, they faced the death penalty.

When the *Scottsboro* case was appealed, the Supreme Court overturned the conviction, saying that the boys had not had a fair trial because there were no blacks on the Alabama grand jury that indicted them. This was one of the first major cases in which the Supreme Court upheld the rights of blacks, and civil libertarians regarded it as a tremendous victory.

However, that was not the end of it. Alabama set up a new grand jury with one black man on it, which promptly reindicted the boys. The case came before the Supreme Court several more times and many groups aided in the blacks' defense, including the NAACP and the ACLU. Eventually, all the convictions were reversed, although the last of the nine was not released from prison until many years later.

After becoming involved in the *Scottsboro* case, the ACLU took on several other cases concerning black rights. It launched an attack on the system of segregated theaters in New Jersey, and tried to eliminate segregation at the American Library Association Convention in Richmond, Virginia.

By 1936, the ACLU and the NAACP were ready to join forces in an attempt to gain voting rights for blacks in a heavily black county in Oklahoma. They had been prevented from voting by the white minority that controlled the area and had the local courts on its side. The issue was brought before the Supreme Court, which ruled that the local courts had to enforce the Constitutional rights of blacks.

In 1938, Charles H. Houston, attorney for the NAACP, joined the Board of Directors of the American Civil Liberties Union. Since then, the two organizations have worked closely together in matters of black rights.

Among the many battles the two groups waged together were the efforts to end segregation in the armed forces; to abolish the "white primary" system that many southern states used for nominating political candidates; to admit blacks into publicly aided housing developments, such as the Stuyvesant Town houses that had been built by the Metropolitan Life Insurance Company in New York; to end anti-Negro clauses in union contracts and housing leases; to pass fair employment practices legislation; and to end the southern poll tax. They cooperated in countless other campaigns to gain equal rights for blacks.

In 1954, a vital breakthrough in securing equal rights for blacks was achieved when the Supreme Court outlawed segregated schools. This had been the NAACP's main goal for many years, and afterwards the organization fought scores of legal battles to end official segregation everywhere—in restaurants, railroad stations, hotels, buses, etc. Pressure by the NAACP and other groups resulted in the passage of the Civil Rights Act of 1957, the first such bill since Reconstruction. In 1964, a stronger civil rights bill was passed, and in 1968 Congress put through a federal fair housing bill. By the late 1960s, the Supreme Court and Congress had just about wiped out the legal basis for discrimination in America. The NAACP was by far the most important organization behind this thrust for black equality, although the ACLU helped out whenever possible.

But the legal gains remained only paper victories until they could actually be enforced in practice. This was the most difficult task of all, for it proved easier to change the laws than to change people's prejudices. Despite the fact that the law was now on their side, blacks still were unable to exercise many of their constitutional and legal rights in the South.

Civil rights workers from the North went down to help, particularly in the job of enforcing black voting rights in southern towns and counties that were politically controlled by whites. Many of these civil rights workers were abused, threatened and sometimes killed by hostile whites who were determined to hang on to power. Newspapers were filled with accounts of these clashes, and it seemed as if everyone's attention was riveted on the South.

In this tense atmosphere, the ACLU in 1964 set up the Lawyers Constitutional Defense Committee to defend civil rights workers and the black community from criminal harassment in Mississippi and Louisiana.

The Committee was based in Jackson, Miss., and had five full-time, paid staff lawyers, plus about 200 volunteer lawyers, mainly white. In 1965, the Committee handled about 3,000 criminal defense suits, ranging from the arrest of 1,100 people in Jackson who had been charged with parading without a permit to the defense of one black who had been accused of raping a white woman.

In doing this work, the Committee lawyers found that they, too, were exposed to danger. One young staff lawyer was shot at by someone in a passing car in West Point, Miss. Fortunately, the assailant was a poor shot, missing his intended target and pelting the side of a house instead.

On another occasion, Alvin Bronstein, who was chief staff counsel in Jackson, was beaten up by three local officials while trying to help his clients. Mr. Bronstein had gone to the Pike County jail in Magnolia, Miss., to arrange for the release of 42 whites and blacks who had been arrested that day during a voter registration rally. But the jailer, a town constable and another uniformed man ganged up on him, assaulting him in the jailhouse.

After he got away, he called the Federal Bureau of Investigation. Then he went back to the jail to demand the release of his clients, and was thrown out again. Finally, the officials let him talk to his clients in the courthouse near the jail.

In these early, turbulent years, the Committee was constantly kept busy protecting the rights of demonstrators who had been arrested by hostile white sheriffs. As Mr. Bronstein said, "We were always trying to get someone out of jail."

However, as this phase of the civil rights movement passed, the Committee lawyers buckled down to the day-to-day, unglamorous and unpublicized task of writing hundreds of legal briefs and filing suits in such matters as job discrimination, racism on draft boards, voting law violations and school segregation.

Even though important legal gains were being made and much was still to be done, the Committee soon faced a new difficulty—people were losing interest in the civil rights movement. Money that had been funneled into the drive for black rights was now being channeled elsewhere—into the peace movement or the environmental protection campaign. It was as if civil rights had been just a temporary fad among liberal "causists," who were now turning their attention elsewhere.

The civil rights movement itself had been split by militant factions, some of which preached violence and expressed anti-white and sometimes anti-Semitic feelings. White liberals, who had provided much of the financial support for the civil rights drive, were both frightened and offended by the black militants. Many of them stopped contributing altogether, while others reduced the size of their donations.

In addition, there was a growing feeling that the battle was actually over in the South, that southern blacks no longer needed much help. Although this was far from true, people believed it, so that those who retained their concern for racial injustice focused more on the Northern cities.

While the public's interest in civil rights was waning, so was the federal government's. The Nixon administration got into office without relying on black votes. In fact, the President had a "southern strategy" designed to lure once-Democratic southern whites to the Republican Party. After he was elected, he adopted a far more relaxed attitude towards civil rights than his predecessors.

Thus, civil rights lawyers found themselves up against public as well as private indifference. In 1970, the Lawyers Constitutional Defense Committee expected to take in less than half the money needed to meet its $150,000 budget. There was a possibility that it would have to close either its Jackson office or its office in New Orleans, La.

If the Committee was unable to meet its expenses, it would have to ask its sponsor, the ACLU, to make up the difference. However, the ACLU, too, was suffering from a shortage of money, as were most other civil rights organizations at the start of the 1970s.

The decline of white interest in the black civil rights movement was reflected in other ways, too. Increasingly, young black lawyers were replacing the white volunteer lawyers who used to flock to the South by the hundreds during the movement's heyday. Now, very few whites come, and many of the early volunteers have gone back to the North.

However, the ACLU is still very active in the South. In recent years it started a new campaign, "Operation Southern Justice," which was a systematic attempt to overhaul the system of justice in the South. In the early stages, the main emphasis of the program was on the integration of juries and of the prison system.

As the ACLU pointed out in its publication, *Civil Liberties,* "The rationale for this approach strikes at the very base of Negro mistrust of the white man's system of justice in the South, where traditionally Negro defendants have not been accorded juries of their peers, and black lawyers have had little chance of successfully defending their clients before unrepresentative juries. The method of accomplishing these ends has involved the use of attorneys who are indigenous to the region, both black and white, and who are courageous enough to initiate the suits necessary to challenge the system."

After much prodding by the ACLU and other groups, the penal systems of Georgia, Alabama and Virginia were integrated. Legal action was also taken to integrate the penal systems of Louisiana, Mississippi and South Carolina.

More recently, "Operation Southern Justice" launched a drive against state policies that were designed to prevent blacks from being elected to public office. One of the first major cases of this type involved the state of Alabama, which had removed 89 black and liberal white candidates from the ballot in 1968. The ACLU challenged the state's action, and the issue came before the Supreme Court in October of that year. The Court reinstated all the candidates, and 17 of them were elected to various public offices throughout Alabama.

The practice of racial discrimination in the North has always been different from that in the South. In the southern states, blacks were segregated by *law* as well as by strict social custom, and southerners were very open about demanding that blacks be kept "in their place."

Discrimination in the North was more subtle but equally

insidious. There were no laws that segregated blacks, but they lived in ghetto slums anyhow, and their children usually wound up in all-black schools. Discrimination was not preached, but it was practiced—by the police, by the courts, by landlords, by employers, by unions and by the schools.

Northerners tended to mask their true feelings, using phrases like, "I have nothing against Negroes, but . . ." This lack of openness only made it more difficult to get a clear picture of racial injustice in the North, or to identify the basic causes of black poverty there.

As long as the drive for black rights was concentrated in the South, northerners were wholly in favor of it. But once the emphasis shifted, it became painfully clear that many northerners were just as reluctant as southerners to permit real integration and equality for blacks. Furthermore, this type of discrimination was extremely hard to fight because it was not a matter of overturning unjust laws, but of changing unjust practices.

After a major policy meeting in 1967, the American Civil Liberties Union decided to set out on a new course—to go into the urban ghettos of the North. The Union planned to set up legal offices that would do nothing but represent ghetto residents in their fight for equal rights. These ghetto offices were to be run by the affiliates, with financial help from the national organization.

At that time, one affiliate already had gone into the ghetto. In 1966, 11 months after the fiery race riots in the Watts section of Los Angeles, the ACLU of Southern California opened an office in Watts. Later on, two more ghetto offices were opened, in East Los Angeles and Venice.

These southern California offices focused solely on police practices in the ghettos. Their main purpose was not to fight court battles but to aid ghetto dwellers in filing complaints about police abuses with the proper officials. Over the last few years, the ghetto offices heard more than 1,000 grievances of various kinds, most of which charged physical mistreatment by the police.

Although the California ghetto offices succeeded in getting people to lodge official complaints against the police, the results were not satisfactory. A report by the southern California branch of the ACLU revealed that out of 165 formal complaints in two years, the police department investigated only 90. Of these, just six were sustained—and the complainants in these six cases never could learn what punishment, if any, had been meted out to the offending policemen.

In a large number of cases, people who were accusing the police of abuses faced criminal charges themselves. Generally, these people were not charged with substantive offenses, like burglary, but only "crimes against police," such as assault on a police officer, resisting arrest or interfering with an officer. Whenever the ACLU lawyers felt that such charges were cover-ups for police malpractices, they would defend the accused in court.

As the ACLU report explained:

> In one way or another, the complainants commit the unwritten crime of "contempt of cop," challenging the authority or actions of the police. Sometimes they ask an officer for his badge number, or protest being frisked. Sometimes they refuse to let officers into their home, demanding to see a search warrant. Sometimes they are flippant, or somehow disrespectful to the officer.
>
> They end up, almost inevitably, in custody, their hands handcuffed behind them. Often when they ask the charges,

the arresting officer concedes he doesn't know, but adds, "We'll think of something."

Early in 1969, the ACLU Foundation of Southern California filed a lawsuit based on the many grievances against the police that had been collected by the ghetto centers, and backed by the statements of hundreds of potential witnesses. The suit, which is still pending, asked the Federal District Court to force an end to police mistreatment of blacks, contending that their civil rights were being violated repeatedly.

Other ACLU ghetto offices have been set up in Chicago, Ill., and Newark, N. J. Their aims are more far-reaching than the southern California offices, for they try to provide legal defense in a wide variety of cases. They are concerned not only with police abuses, but with other types of unjust treatment of ghetto residents.

For example, the Chicago ghetto office has gone to court on behalf of several "contract buyers"—people who sign a contract to buy a home, usually for about twice what it's worth. They are willing to buy their homes on monthly installments because they do not have the money for a down payment and cannot get a bank mortgage. They do not own the proprety and they have no safeguards. If they miss one payment at any time, they may be dispossessed.

When the Chicago ghetto office learned that growing numbers of black contract buyers were being evicted from their homes—some after making payments for 10 years—ACLU lawyers launched a number of successful lawsuits on their behalf.

Nevertheless, in all the ghetto law offices, police malpractices are the major concern. Ghetto residents tend to think of the police as their enemy, and very often they are reluctant to report crimes or cooperate with the police in any way. Relations between the police and ghetto dwellers are marked by mutual fear and distrust—an attitude that is not likely to change as long as the police show less respect for the constitutional rights of blacks than of whites. For example, in white neighborhoods, police almost never stop and frisk someone without very good cause, but in the ghettos it happens all the time. Blacks are well aware of this, and it only serves to lessen their respect for the law.

Both the ACLU and the NAACP have always felt that black rights can best be achieved in an integrated society. The two civil rights groups dedicated years of service and large sums of money to the cause of integration, and since the 1950s their efforts have been fruitful, at least in a legal sense.

That is why it was painful for these organizations to face the fact that, by the late 1960s, growing numbers of militant young blacks were rejecting the goal of integration. They had waited long enough for it, and were tired of empty legal victories that promised them much but did them little good in practice. The black separatist movement branched out in several directions, and one of its major goals was to gain black control over black schools, rather than continuing the fight for integrated schools.

The separatists felt that blacks were getting nowhere with their campaign for integrated classrooms; most schools still remained heavily imbalanced years after the Supreme Court had outlawed segregation. Meanwhile, a great many black children were still coming out of the ghetto schools barely able to read or write. These schools, which were administered mainly by whites, were not reaching the ghetto youngsters—and the black militants claimed they weren't really trying.

Instead of waiting for that far-off day when schools might actually be integrated, the militants demanded improvement of black schools *now,* and insisted that they be placed under the control of the ghetto community. They felt that neighborhood school boards should have power to hire and fire teachers, choose principals and decide upon the curriculum. Above all, they wanted more flexibility in the school system so they could experiment with various methods of teaching black children.

The idea of community control over ghetto schools was taken up by many black groups, even those that still saw integration as their eventual goal. Largely because of these demands, New York City in 1968 set up two experimental school districts in ghetto areas that had a small measure of autonomy, although not as much as black community leaders had wanted.

Controversy flared almost at once. When one of the experimental districts apparently overstepped its powers and fired a number of white teachers, the teachers' union went on strike, paralyzing the entire New York City school system. The teachers had been wary of community control in the first place, and the dismissals only hardened their opposition.

In the conflict over who was right—the teachers or the black educators and community leaders—New Yorkers wound up fighting each other bitterly. The New York Civil Liberties Union was almost torn apart by the conflict. Many members felt that the teachers' union was right in trying to protect its members from arbitrary and unfair dismissals, and demanded that the NYCLU take a stand supporting the rights of labor.

But others in the affiliate believed that urgent new priorities were at stake in this dispute that overshadowed the labor issue. They felt it was so important to improve the quality of ghetto schools that black administrators were right in dismissing teachers who, they felt, did not sympathize with their aims. Also, these teachers were not actually "fired," but transferred out of the experimental district. They could have been placed in other schools, if the teachers' union and the Board of Education had agreed.

The dispute boiled down to a matter of black power vs. union power, complicated by the fact that the majority of teachers in the union were both white and Jewish. This led to outbursts of anti-Semitism on the part of blacks, and growing anti-black feeling on the part of Jews. Since the NYCLU itself was mainly white and Jewish, feelings ran very high.

But even without this complication, it was a cruel dilemma. Civil libertarians faced a bitter choice between supporting the rights of labor or supporting the rights of blacks who were trying to improve their children's education. In the end, the NYCLU supported the black groups, but the affiliate still carries the scars of this internal battle.

One year later, the national ACLU came out in favor of "school decentralization and community control efforts throughout the country" as a means of enlarging educational opportunities for minority groups. However, the Union said, such programs must protect the rights of students, parents and teachers.

This announcement came after many months of intense study by the ACLU. The Union stated:

> In taking this action, we do not abandon integration as the eventual goal. Indeed, we view integration as an ideal condition for educational equality, and we will continue to fight for it.
>
> However, if we are to achieve the civil liberties goal of equality, it is time to face the fact that integration efforts over the past 15 years have produced wholly inadequate results. Civil rights legislation and court rulings have

established in law the principle of equality under the 14th amendment to the U. S. Constitution, but they have done little to implement the fact of equality in the lives of most blacks, Puerto Ricans and Mexican-Americans in this country. Despite open housing laws, busing programs and the like, most schools still are heavily white or heavily nonwhite. And it is demonstrable that "separate" has not been "equal."

In many communities, particularly in the urban ghettos, the stark fact is that we will continue to have segregated public schools. New strategies for equalizing educational opportunity are imperative lest we write off still another generation of minority children. We cannot afford the price of such patience.

The ACLU noted that community control of schools would not solve all problems, but at least it promised "real progress toward achieving meaningful equality." Decentralization was a way of breaking the rigidity of aloof school bureaucracies, fostering parental concern and providing better supervision of teachers and administrators, the ACLU said.

In alluding to the New York City conflict over teachers' rights, the Union noted, "Some believe these rights cannot be reconciled with the new forms of school control. We disagree." They are compatible, the ACLU said, "if the criteria of accountability are clearly drawn, fairly negotiated and objectively applied."

However, the Union emphasized, "the right of children to learn" was most important of all.

As the black civil rights movement grew more militant in the late 1960s and early 1970s, it alienated many of its white supporters. White liberals could sympathize with the aims but not the methods of groups like the Black Panthers, who urged blacks to fight for their rights with guns.

The ACLU has never supported the use of violence to protest unjust laws or practices, feeling that it only brings on violence or repression in return. Nevertheless, the Union upholds the right of groups like the Panthers to *advocate* anything they please, and to be punished only for crimes they actually commit, not for the things they say. Similarly, the Union feels that these groups have the right to meet or carry on peaceful activities without interference from the police.

In a study it made a few years ago, the ACLU concluded that police across the country were systematically harassing the Black Panthers. Since that time, there have been several police shoot-outs with the Panthers, resulting in many deaths. The most notorious of these incidents was when the Chicago police raided Panther headquarters in the middle of the night, killing Fred Hampton, chairman of the Illinois Black Panthers, and Mark Clark, another member of the Party. The police claimed that the Panthers shot at them first, but there was evidence that the Panthers were killed in their beds.

The case was closed after an investigation by the police and coroner's jury placed the blame on the Panthers. However, this report conflicted with a federal grand jury report that said the police fired 99 shots and the Panthers fired just one. The Illinois Civil Liberties Union refused to let the issue rest, and finally succeeded in having the investigation reopened.

Now the ACLU is on the alert regarding the Panther's rights —particularly their right to exist, but also their right to assemble peacefully, speak in public, distribute literature and get fair trials when charged with crimes. When several Black Panthers were on trial for murder in New Haven, Conn., the ACLU hired a lawyer to work full-time on the civil liberties aspects of the trial to make sure that political prejudice against the Panthers did not spill over into the courtroom.

In Louisiana, the ACLU was instrumental in finding lawyers for members of the Black Panther Party who were arrested on charges of attempted murder after a gun battle with the police. The Panthers had not been able to find anyone to defend them. The ACLU only defends people whose rights have been violated; it does not usually handle criminal defense, but it will make sure that defendants are properly represented by an attorney.

In another case, the ACLU came to the defense of several Black Panthers in New York who apparently had been enticed into commiting illegal acts by a police undercover agent. The facts in the case were as follows:

In August 1969, a car containing three Panthers and the agent was stopped in New York City. The Panthers were arrested and charged with conspiracy to rob a hotel, conspiracy to murder, attempted robbery, attempted murder of a policeman at the time of arrest and possession of weapons.

But ACLU lawyers showed that the car had been supplied for the Panthers by the police, that the agent had drawn a map of the hotel, that the agent had suggested stealing a car and "casing" the hotel and that the agent had offered to obtain weapons for the Panthers on a number of other occasions.

After a long trial, the jury found that the Panthers had been "entrapped." They were acquitted of all charges except possession of a sawed-off shotgun and a red pepper spray.

Recently, the ACLU has been involved in a wide variety of cases concerning black rights. For example, the ACLU is defending the right of black servicemen to wear Afro hairstyles, claiming that it is their way of expressing racial and cultural pride—and that such expression is protected by the First Amendment.

One of the most bitter complaints of black citizens is that they are frequently suspected of crimes without valid reason, and are subjected to illegal searches in their homes. When they complain about such treatment, they are either ignored or abused. In Plainfield, N. J., in the summer of 1967, unknown thieves stole 46 semi-automatic rifles from the Plainfield Machine Company. Governor Richard Hughes, invoking his emergency powers, suspended the Fourth Amendment, which protects people against unreasonable searches and seizures. After that, armed troopers and guardsmen went on a raid of blacks' homes throughout Plainfield.

The raiders destroyed property and abused and humiliated the blacks. One woman was sitting at home nursing her six-week-old baby when the police broke in. Another man's home was torn apart in the search for the stolen rifles.

No stolen weapons were found in any of the homes. Apparently, local officials hadn't really expected to find anything, but wanted to show their white constituents that the police were on the job. Leo Kaplowitz, the county prosecutor, was quoted by the *Washington Post* as saying at the time of the raids, "You don't think for a minute you expect to find guns, do you? The search is a symbol of law and order, and it is vitally important for this community to see that symbol."

The New Jersey affiliate of the ACLU filed a suit for $1 million in damages and an injunction on behalf of 66 blacks whose homes had been partially wrecked. Defendants included the city and state police and the state National Guard, their chief officers and former Governor Richard Hughes.

The Federal District Court supported the blacks' claims,

awarding them $19,000 in the lawsuit and enjoining the defendants from conducting such searches as long as they held office.

In supporting the black struggle for equal rights and opportunities, the American Civil Liberties Union has come a long way from its non-intervention policy of 50 years ago. But this change has reflected the changing attitude of America as a whole, for 50 years ago most white Americans gave no thought at all to the idea of equality for blacks.

This is hardly true today. A nation that was once indifferent to the race problem is now being torn apart by it. Fear, anger and concern have replaced the indifference. The drive for black rights is now very high on the ACLU's list of priorities because the organization feels that the need to find peaceful solutions to racial conflicts has become urgent—otherwise, the whole nation may erupt in violence, threatening the rights and freedoms of all Americans.

[5]
SPEAKING OUT ON THE FAR RIGHT

What makes the ACLU unique is that it is willing to defend causes it hates—for free—providing a matter of civil liberties is at stake.

Over the last 40 years, the ACLU has often come to the aid of fanatical right-wing or racist groups whose rights were violated. Defending such unpopular groups is a difficult and unrewarding chore. Every time the ACLU goes to court on behalf of the American Nazi Party or the Ku Klux Klan, it angers many of its own liberal supporters, who are more sympathetic towards the left than towards the far right. But the ACLU has stuck rigidly to its policy of championing civil rights for *all,* not just for those whose ideas it may prefer.

This non-partisan policy was first put to the test back in 1930, when the American Fascist Association and Order of Black Shirts was founded in Atlanta, Georgia. According to the group's charter, its purposes were "to inculcate and foster in the minds of its members and the public generally white supremacy, the obedience to law and order, to disseminate patriotism and loyalty to the government of the United States and to assist its members in finding employment." The group offered black shirts for sale at $5 each.

When a branch of this group tried to hold a public meeting

in Macon, Ga., the mayor of the town prevented them on the grounds that they might create a riot.

Much to everyone's surprise, the American Civil Liberties Union came to the fascists' defense. At that time, the ACLU was widely regarded as a left-wing organization because it had defended the rights of so many communists, anarchists, labor organizers, socialists and pacifists.

But from 1930 on, the Union has also stepped forward to protect the rights and freedoms of those on the radical right, such as the Minutemen and the late George Lincoln Rockwell and his American Nazi Party. It even aided one of its fiercest enemies, Senator Joseph McCarthy. When the Senate set up a committee to study the possibility of censuring Senator McCarthy, the ACLU insisted that McCarthy be granted a right he had denied to others—the right to confront and cross-examine the witnesses against him.

One of the most important—and unpopular—cases handled by the ACLU in recent years involved the National States' Rights Party, a white supremacist group. The controversy began on a hot August evening in 1966, when party members were holding a public rally near the courthouse steps in Princess Anne, Maryland. Inside the courthouse, two blacks were being held on charges of raping a white woman.

The Party speakers had set up an amplified public address system, and their voices boomed out over an area of several blocks. As the rally gathered momentum, the crowd milling around in the streets swelled from about 50 people to more than 200. About 25 percent of this audience was black.

During the course of the rally, the speakers talked about black people in highly insulting and inflammatory language. One spokesman ranted, "I'm going to tell you niggers out there now the best thing you can do is start taking reservations for Africa. Get ready to leave this country. This is a white man's country. Princess Anne is a white man's town. This is a white man's county." He also suggested that blacks could have a choice of transportation to Africa, including "in a box." Other speakers insulted Jews, too, but most of their venom was directed at blacks.

The blacks in the audience were visibly disturbed and angry at their remarks, but remained peaceful throughout the rally. Most of the white people there seemed friendly towards the speakers. Although the speakers were fiercely hostile to blacks, they did not incite the crowd to violence, and no violence erupted at any time.

When the rally ended at about 8:30 PM, one speaker told the crowd, "I want you to . . . be back here at the same time tomorrow night, bring every friend you have. . . . Come on back tomorrow night; let's raise a little bit of hell for the white race."

The next morning, local officials went to court and got a temporary injunction barring any rallies by the National States' Rights Party in Somerset County, Maryland, for the next 10 days. The purpose was to prevent the danger of riots or civil disorders that might result from the inflammatory speeches. The Party did not have a chance to defend itself at a hearing before the order was issued; members were simply notified that they could not meet in public. Later on, there was a hearing to determine if the ban should be extended for a longer period of time. States' Rights Party members had a chance to speak at this hearing, but the decision went against them anyhow. The ban was extended to 10 months.

When the Party tried to get legal help, it found that few

people were willing to come to its aid. According to an affidavit by Joseph Carroll, Field Director of the National States' Rights Party,

> I contacted an attorney, John Brackenbrough Fox . . . of Baltimore, Maryland, who had on other occasions represented clients in opposition to local integration laws in Baltimore. Mr. Fox refused to take our case in Somerset County because he felt that "we were too hot" and that the case would be harmful to his practice and his reputation.
>
> On 8/9/66, I then contacted another attorney, George Washington Williams . . . who had been very active in "conservative causes" and who at one time proposed to one of the local Bar Associations an amendment to the U. S. Constitution calling for the abolition of the 14th amendment. Mr. Williams declined to represent us in Somerset County without specifically stating his reasons.
>
> In desperation, I formally requested the local chapter of the ACLU to represent us on 8/10/66, and met with the representatives of the local chapter on 8/11/66, and after this meeting I was told that the full legal panel would have to meet in what could be described as an emergency session and decide whether to represent us or not. . . .

In what must have been a very difficult decision, the Maryland affiliate of the ACLU agreed to defend the white supremacist group since the case involved what seemed to be a clear violation of the right of freedom of speech. "Freedom for the thought we hate" is an easy slogan to say, but in actual practice few "respectable" people are willing to defend the rights of very unsavory groups. Partly this is out of fear that the public may assume they share the group's beliefs, and rather than be "tainted" this way, they do not get involved.

The ACLU has not shied away from such situations, keeping in mind that its real client is the Bill of Rights itself, and it just doesn't matter what individuals are involved.

In defending the right of all groups to speak freely, the ACLU follows the guidelines set down by Supreme Court Associate Justice Louis D. Brandeis in 1927. In a dissent from the majority, Justice Brandeis said, "No danger flowing from speech can be deemed 'clear and present' unless" the evil is so imminent that it may occur "before there is opportunity for full discussion." Thus, as Justice Holmes once said, falsely shouting "Fire!" in a crowded theater would not be permissible because it might create panic before there was time to find out the facts. But where there is a time lapse between the speech and the danger that may result from it, the speech is protected by the Constitution.

In the ACLU view, even such extreme speech as advocating armed rebellion "tomorrow" should be allowed because the danger would not arise immediately and directly from the speech; there would be time for thought.

The ACLU's interpretation of the First Amendment is broader than that of the Supreme Court, so that the organization is continually involved in cases that press for greater freedom of speech. In the case of the States' Rights Party, the Maryland Court of Appeals agreed with the ACLU argument that a 10-month ban on Party rallies was unjustified.

The Court said that 10 months was an unreasonable length of time, and that it was "arbitrary to assume that a clear and present danger of civil disturbance and riot would persist for 10 months." However, the Court did uphold the 10-day ban on Party rallies.

This decision did not satisfy the American Civil Liberties Union, which wanted courts to end the practice of barring speeches or rallies *in advance,* even when violence is threatened. The ACLU is particularly opposed to this type of prior restraint of speech, feeling that it is clearly unconstitutional. In continuing the battle, the ACLU took the case up to the Supreme Court.

In the fall of 1968, the *Carroll* case reached the High Court. Arguing on behalf of the white supremacist group was a pretty, black ACLU lawyer with an Afro hairstyle and dangling earrings, Eleanor Holmes Norton, then the assistant legal director of the American Civil Liberties Union.

Mrs. Norton won the case, although on narrower grounds than the ACLU would have liked. Speaking for the majority, Associate Justice Abe Fortas declared that it was unconstitutional for courts to delay public meetings, even when violence was threatened, without first hearing testimony from those who wished to meet.

This decision upset the long-standing practice of judges issuing temporary restraining orders solely on the testimony of a complainer. They were called ex-parte (one-sided) orders. The decision meant that unless a group was given a chance to argue its case before the judge, he could not prevent them from speaking.

As Justice Fortas explained, prior restraint of speech is a very serious matter, and "there is a danger in relying exclusively on the version of events and dangers presented by prosecuting officials because of their special interests."

The ACLU and other civil liberties groups would have liked the Court to go further than this—to come out with an *absolute* ban on blocking speeches or rallies in advance—so this was only a partial victory. Nevertheless, it was an important one, since *all* controversial groups and individuals gained greater free speech protection because of it.

Defending a group of white supremacists could not have been easy for Mrs. Norton, who admits that she is happiest when defending people whose views she shares. Nevertheless, she has gone to court on behalf of several racist groups, including the Ku Klux Klan and Alabama Governor George Wallace's party. But it was only in the *Carroll* case that Mrs. Norton had direct contact with one of the defendants.

"I didn't handle the case at the trial level, only at the Appeals Court and the Supreme Court where the defendant's presence is not required," Mrs. Norton recalled in an interview with *Ebony* magazine in January 1969. "I was therefore very surprised when William Zenman, my co-counsel, told me that one of the NSRP's most rabid racists was in the courtroom. My first reaction was to completely avoid him, thereby not embarrassing him. After all, I had gotten the case not because I am black, but due to a request from our Maryland affiliate for assistance. Melvin Wulf, our legal director, was out of town, so I had to go. I didn't want the young man to feel that the ACLU was making fun of him.

"Well, I was besieged by the defendant who ran up to me of his own volition, putting out his hand to shake mine, exclaiming that I had done an excellent job and that I'd shown 'lots of guts' in taking their case. I quickly explained that it had nothing to do with guts. It was simply my organization's commitment to the First Amendment. He just smiled. I still don't know if he realized what I was saying."

In explaining how she can defend white racists, Mrs. Norton says there are certain principles she believes in very strongly. "One is racial equality. The other is free speech." To promote racial equality, she has been very active in the civil rights movement. To promote free speech, "I represent *anyone* whose free speech has been infringed."

Mrs. Norton points out, "The ACLU believes that a person has the right to put forth whatever ideas he holds, even if they are obnoxious, so long as he doesn't, in the course of putting them forth, incite immediate violence." Defining immediate violence, she says, "It occurs when a speech makes people ready to go out immediately to commit violence and there is no time in the interval to persuade them not to do so. It must be a clear and present danger. That doesn't mean in the future. It means right now. None of my cases have come to that point. That's why they had to be vigorously defended."

In one of these free speech cases, Mrs. Norton defended George Wallace's right to hold a political rally in New York City's Shea Stadium during his 1968 third-party campaign for the presidency.

"To deny him this right would have set a bad precedent," Mrs. Norton said. "It could have been used against any political group, even one that I might agree with."

Mrs. Norton won the case for George Wallace, basing her argument on constitutional grounds. Although she did not have to deal with Mr. Wallace directly, she did have to work with his aides. Describing her relations with them, she says they were "entirely civil as one might expect in a situation of this kind, making no ironic remarks whatsoever. Wallace has around him a kind of Harvard-educated, Southern aristocratic type I have known before. They are prepared to meet any surprise without revealing it to be that."

Noting that she took on the Wallace case deliberately, she said, "I did it because I believe in the principle of free speech, though to be truthful, there was some ironic malice aforethought as well."

The third case, one that Mrs. Norton felt was "atrocious," involved a member of the Ku Klux Klan who had been convicted of criminal syndicalism—a doctrine advocating the overthrow of the government by violence. The criminal syndicalism laws are vaguely-worded statutes that are on the books in almost every state. They are used mainly against left-wingers. In the 1930s, they were frequently used to jail labor leaders who were organizing strikes. In the 1960s they were used against some black leaders, notably William Epton, who was allegedly involved in the Harlem riots in New York City in 1964.

The Klansman who was convicted of criminal syndicalism had staged a televised rally to announce that the Klan was planning a march on Washington and on three southern states. He said that they were going down there to tell the President, Congress and the Supreme Court the things they felt needed to be changed. For this he was convicted, given one to 10 years and fined $1,000.

In appealing his conviction, Mrs. Norton emphasized, "This is a situation where a Klansman may well win a case whose greatest benefactors will be black militants and other radicals rather than the right wing."

How does the black community feel about Mrs. Norton's defense of racists in free speech cases? "I have been pleased with the reception that I have received from my black friends," she says, "including black militants. The typical response I get is, 'I couldn't do it, but I see the point of your doing it.' They understand that if we ever get to the point in this country where a person can go to jail just for what he says, black militants will be the first to go down. I am glad they understand this because I have a stake in the black struggle and want my cohorts in the struggle to understand the role I am playing."

However, not all of them do. When Mrs. Norton was invited to speak at a college in New York City, a few of the militant black students there were not at all pleased. They could not forgive her for having defended George Wallace's right to speak at Shea Stadium. When asked how they felt about the principle of free speech, one of them replied: "We can't think about free speech for racists. It's too late for that."

This is an attitude that the ACLU and Mrs. Norton consider terribly dangerous, for if the Bill of Rights is not applied equally to all, in the end it may be applied to none.

In 1970, Mrs. Norton was named Chairman of the New York City Commission on Human Rights. As such, she no longer has any connection with the ACLU, although her attitudes and activities epitomize everything the Union stands for.

The number and strength of ultra-right-wing groups grew during the 1960s, focusing attention on such movements as the John Birch Society, the Rev. Billy James Hargis' Christian Crusade and the Rev. Carl McIntire and his Faith Theological Seminary. As these groups entered the limelight, their liberal opponents tried to reduce their influence and curtail their activities—sometimes treading on their constitutional rights in the process. Because of this, the ACLU became involved in more ultra-right-wing cases during the 1960s than during any other period in its history.

At the same time, it also found on several occasions that it had to battle a number of liberal organizations who used to work very closely with the ACLU. One such battle occurred in 1965, when the ACLU defended the right of Faith Theological Seminary to buy a radio station in Pennsylvania.

The Seminary is a religious institution led by an outspoken, extreme right-winger, the Rev. Carl McIntire. Mr. McIntire is against civil rights legislation, opposes the United Nations and has accused the National Council of Churches of having "leftist tendencies." When his Seminary tried to acquire the radio station, more than 40 religious, labor and human relations groups asked the Federal Communications Commission to bar the sale. The National Association for the Advancement of Colored People, the Anti-Defamation League of B'nai B'rith and the Greater Philadelphia Council of Churches, among many others, feared that the Rev. McIntire would use the radio station to fan racial and religious hatred, and to spread his fanatical right-wing philosophy.

But the American Civil Liberties Union did not join in the protests. On the contrary, it appealed to the FCC to ignore the protests and to approve the Seminary's acquisition of radio station WXUR. To bar it, the ACLU felt, would mean that the government was passing judgment on the social value of the Seminary's opinions. This, said Spencer Coxe, executive director of the Pennsylvania affiliate of the ACLU, would be "government censorship."

The Union asked the FCC only to make sure that the Seminary adhered to the "fairness doctrine," which requires each radio station to permit the airing of diverse points of view. If the Seminary violated the doctrine, Mr. Coxe said, then its license should be revoked. But he added that the FCC should not assume in advance that the Seminary would run the radio station on a totally one-sided basis.

"Just because Rev. McIntire has said hideous things in the

past doesn't mean he'll run his station unfairly," Mr. Coxe said during the height of the controversy.

However, the Jewish Community Relations Council, an old ally of the ACLU, felt quite differently about the matter. The JCRC did not want the Seminary to take over the radio station because the "Rev. McIntire would have three years to spout off his extremist views before his license could be reviewed," according to Jules Cohen, executive director of the group. "During that time he could say anything he wanted. And once granted, it's almost impossible to revoke a license."

He pointed out that Rev. McIntire had been broadcasting over more than 600 radio stations across the country, and that the Jewish Community Relations Council was not trying to deny his free speech rights. "But nobody has a constitutional right to a radio station," Mr. Cohen said. "There's a matter of public interest involved."

The fact that the Council and the ACLU were on opposite sides in this fight was painful to both of them. They had been long-time allies, and were still cooperating on many other causes. However, they had come to a parting of the ways over the issue of defending the rights of extremists.

Speaking of this split, Mr. Cohen said, "I think very highly of the ACLU. If it didn't exist it would have to be created. But at times I think it's too purist and impractical, and fails to take into account real-life situations."

Fighting with its old liberal friends is hard for the ACLU but sometimes necessary for the sake of civil liberties. "I'm not saying liberals are abandoning civil liberties. They're not," said Mr. Coxe. "But the emergence of extreme right-wing groups has produced more occasions where liberals are tempted to sacrifice civil liberties for other values they hold dear. As a result, we've had to part company from many of our liberal friends to a degree we never had to 10 years ago.

"Even though labels are deceptive, I still think conservatives are worse than liberals when it comes to violating civil liberties," Mr. Coxe went on. "But these days you do hear more liberals using some of the same arguments McCarthyites used in the early 1950s. That is, some tend to argue that it is legitimate to quiet extreme right-wing groups on the grounds such groups don't exercise free speech, but abuse it. That's the same argument McCarthy used. Certainly, some liberals tend to depart from strict civil liberties positions when their own ox is gored."

The ACLU won the battle to allow Faith Theological Seminary to acquire a radio station in Pennsylvania. The FCC agreed that to withhold a license would mean the government was prejudging the Seminary.

However, after the radio station had been in operation for a while, new charges were filed against it. The FCC upheld a hearing examiner's report that the station had, in fact, violated the "fairness doctrine" and committed other abuses. The ACLU has been studying these new developments.

Among the other right-wing groups that the ACLU has aided is the John Birch Society, a nationwide group whose activities are sometimes cloaked in secrecy and whose leader once accused both President Eisenhower and former Chief Justice Earl Warren of being communist dupes.

When 15 policemen in Philadelphia were discovered to be members of the John Birch Society, the mayor threatened disciplinary action against them. But the American Civil Liberties Union came to the policemen's defense, offering to assist them in case any action was taken. The Union felt the men had a right to belong to any organization they wished, and that their effectiveness as policemen should be judged only by their performance on the job, not by their outside activities.

The ACLU also came out against a New Jersey bill that was directed against the activities of the Ku Klux Klan. The bill would have made it a crime to "burn, deface, mutilate or otherwise desecrate a cross or other religious symbol." The measure was aimed at the Klan's well-known penchant for burning crosses to terrorize its enemies and call attention to itself.

The ACLU's stand in this matter was exactly the same as its position regarding flag desecration laws—that they are unconstitutional because the mutilation of a flag (or a cross) is a symbolic form of speech. Thus, it is protected by the First Amendment.

Emil Oxfeld, president of the New Jersey affiliate of the ACLU, called the anti-cross-burning bill an infringement on free speech. "One infringement leads to another," he said. "The lesson of history is that the meaning of liberty is indivisible. If the legislature pares down one group's means of communicating its ideas today, then tomorrow it will cut down the rights of another group.

"A bill of this kind is clothed with righteousness because the content of the Klan's speech is understandably offensive to many people. But the answer to the denial of equal protection of the laws suffered by the Negro community is not by passing a law of this kind."

The ACLU also angered some of its liberal followers in several other cases: when it came to the aid of the late George Lincoln Rockwell, head of the American Nazi Party, after he was denied a permit to speak in Union Square in New York

City; when it insisted that the *National Review*, a conservative weekly, should be allowed to rent the facilities of New York City's Hunter College for public meetings; and when it supported the request of Mississippi's segregationist governor, Ross Barnett, for a jury trial in the contempt of court case brought against him by the federal government.

These cases and many others clearly demonstrate the ACLU's zealousness in defense of civil rights—*anyone's* civil rights. They also show that the cause of civil rights, like politics, sometimes makes strange bedfellows.

[6]
BIG BROTHER IS WATCHING YOU

In April 1965, the following advertisement appeared in *Esquire* magazine:

THE SNOOPER

$18.95 (Lincoln Electronics, N. Y. C.)

Amplifies sound 1,000,000 times
World's only private listening device
- Aim it at a group of friends a block away and hear every word!
- An outgrowth of the fabulous missile-tracking antennas.
- Transistorized. Weighs only 4 pounds.

Incredible as it may seem, it does amplify sound 1,000,000 times. Sensitive 18″ disk reflector will pick up normal conversations at a distance (500 feet) where you can't even see lips moving. Just think of the ways you can use this.

Portable; complete with tripod and stethoscopic earphones.

The best part—a regular tape recorder can be plugged into the back to take everything down. Have fun!

In the same issue of *Esquire,* there was another ad for an eavesdropping device:

International Audio-Wall Probe

Just place against any wall, pick up sounds, voices in the next room. . . . Amazing little device is equipped with suction-cup ultra-high-gain amplifier that you simply place against the wall and through stethoscopic earphones you can detect the faintest of voices and sounds in the next room—Good for knowing what the kids are doing without their realizing it! You can hook the Audio Wall Probe into your tape recorder.

$49.95 $6.95 for earphones

Another ad also appeared in the same issue:

Dual Listening Device

This light compact instrument permits two or more people to listen in on a phone conversation without the other party knowing it. . . . A fun buy for $4.75.

Modern technology has made it possible for the general public to buy such snooping devices at very reasonable prices. Although it is alarming enough to think that your friends or neighbors may be using these devices just for the fun of it, it is far more frightening to realize that the government, too, may be using them at any time.

Agencies like the Federal Bureau of Investigation, the Central Intelligence Agency, Army Intelligence and other investigative units have highly sophisticated electronic spying equipment that they may use to gather information about suspected criminals, traitors, revolutionaries or anyone else under surveillance. Although there are laws regulating the use of such devices, the temptation for the government to use them freely is very strong—especially during periods when the country is plagued by dissent and turmoil.

This brings up a fundamental problem of modern society: to what extent, if any, is the government's power to track down lawbreakers limited by the people's right to privacy?

Complicating this question is the fact that the right of privacy is not mentioned anywhere in the Constitution. At the time the document was drawn up, there were no such things as electronic spying devices that could seriously threaten people's privacy. There were no telephones to be tapped; there were no cameras to be concealed; there were no tape recorders to take down conversations; there were no microfilm files in which vast quantities of information about people could be stored in a relatively small space. In short, with nothing of this type to jeopardize the right of privacy, there was no reason for the framers of the Constitution to specifically guarantee this right or even to think of it at all.

Because of this omission, legal scholars today disagree as to whether a right of privacy can be *inferred* from other articles of the Constitution. Among those who say no is Hugo Black, Associate Justice of the Supreme Court. Justice Black feels that no matter how desirable the right of privacy may be, it isn't mentioned at all in the Constitution and isn't guaranteed.

Taking the opposite position in the debate is Supreme Court Justice William O. Douglas, who believes that many of the provisions of the Bill of Rights, taken together, create "zones of privacy." In recent years, the Court majority has tended to go along more with Justice Douglas than with Justice Black. In the 1965 case of *Griswold vs. Connecticut,* the Supreme Court held that Connecticut's ban on the sale and use of contraceptives was unconstitutional because it violated the people's right of privacy. However, the "right of privacy" is still a somewhat fuzzy legal concept that has to be worked out on a case-by-case basis.

The American Civil Liberties Union fully supports Justice Douglas' view that the Bill of Rights creates "zones of privacy," and has flatly opposed any kind of electronic eavesdropping by the government. The Union's position can best be summed up by quoting Supreme Court Justice Louis Brandeis' ringing dissent in *Olmstead vs. United States*. This was a 1928 case that concerned the government's use of wiretapping to obtain evidence against racketeers, despite a federal law against wiretapping. The Court majority upheld the validity of the evidence against the racketeers even though the wiretap itself was illegal, but Justice Brandeis strongly disagreed. He stated:

> The makers of our Constitution undertook to secure conditions favorable to the pursuit of happiness. They recognized the significance of man's spiritual nature, his feelings, and of his intellect. They knew that only a part of the pain, pleasures and satisfactions of life are to be found in material things. They sought to protect Americans in their beliefs, their thoughts, their emotions and their sensations. They conferred, as against the government, the right to be let alone—the most comprehensive of rights and a right most valued by civilized man. To protect that right, every unjustifiable intrusion by the government upon the privacy of the individual, whatever the means employed, must be deemed a violation of the Fourth Amendment.

(This amendment guarantees the right of the people to be secure in their persons, houses, papers and effects, against unreasonable searches and seizures.)

Furthermore, Justice Brandeis said that if the government used evidence against people that was obtained by tapping their telephone conversations, it would violate the Fifth Amendment guarantee that no person "shall be compelled in any criminal case to be a witness against himself."

In this way, a "right of privacy" was inferred from the Fourth and Fifth Amendments, even though it was not specifically mentioned in the Bill of Rights.

The ACLU also feels that a "right of privacy" can be inferred from the First Amendment's guarantee of freedom of speech; the Third Amendment's guarantee against the quartering of soldiers in people's homes without their consent; and the Ninth Amendment's provision that "The enumeration in the Constitution of certain rights, shall not be construed to deny or disparage others retained by the people."

Despite the fact that a constitutional "right of privacy" is rapidly gaining legal support, it has been very hard to curb governmental invasion of privacy. For example, in 1966 it was revealed that the FBI had far more eavesdropping powers than most people realized.

For many years, the FBI was allowed to tap telephone wires only in matters involving national security or "danger to human life." Even then, FBI Director J. Edgar Hoover had to get the express consent of the Attorney General before tapping any citizen's telephone. This regulation was in effect since 1940.

However, during this same period, there were no limitations on Mr. Hoover's power to use *other* electronic eavesdropping devices in matters of "national safety, including organized crime, kidnapping and matters wherein human life might be at stake." This meant that Mr. Hoover could order apartments or offices "bugged" without permission from anyone else —a fact that was not known to the general public until 1966, when the tax evasion case of Fred B. Black, Jr., came before the Supreme Court.

Evidence against Black had been obtained by means of an FBI listening device (not a telephone tap) that was placed in Black's hotel room for about three months in 1963. Among the conversations that the FBI overheard in this way were private talks between Black and the lawyer who was defending him against tax evasion charges, for which he was later convicted. In addition, Black's case did not involve "organized crime, kidnapping" or matters endangering human life, so the FBI "bug" violated the guidelines Mr. Hoover was supposed to follow. But since there was no one to overrule Mr. Hoover, he was actually free to use "bugging" devices whenever he pleased.

However, by the time this became public knowledge, the practice had already been stopped. In June 1965, President Lyndon Johnson had barred *all* federal departments and agencies from using eavesdropping devices, such as hidden microphones, except in national security cases—and then only with the permission of the Attorney General.

This policy of respect for the right of privacy was strictly followed during the Johnson administration. However, when Richard Nixon took over as President, and appointed John Mitchell as Attorney General, the right of privacy was subordinated to the goal of law and order.

Under the 1968 Crime Control and Safe Streets Bill, Congress gave federal, state and local agencies broad powers to use wiretapping, bugging and electronic eavesdropping devices. Attorney General Mitchell announced his intention to make good use of these devices, and apparently has been true to his word.

The American Civil Liberties Union came out strongly against this new policy. In January 1969, the Union declared: "It is our contention that the wiretap provisions of the 1968 Act and Mr. Mitchell's stated intention to broaden the use of them are dangerous, heavy-handed intrusions by the government into the private lives of individuals and we intend to seize every possible opportunity to challenge and test them until they are overturned."

Electronic eavesdropping is not the only type of intrusion on privacy that the ACLU is trying to prevent. Our advanced technology is enabling the government to put together a massive surveillance system, including computerized files on citizens who have engaged in "political dissent" or "civil disorders." A huge quantity of information is being recorded on microfilms, tapes and memory cores. According to the ACLU, this sophisticated machinery for the maintenance of personal dossiers on a great many Americans is a concept that is "odious" to a free society.

Nevertheless, many government agencies have set up their own surveillance systems. Together they have been installing about 500 computers a year, most of which will be used to store information about citizens. All arrests and conviction records from the 50 states are expected to be put into a central computer. The Secret Service has a massive file on persons who have spoken out strongly against national policy, and it keeps these people under surveillance when the President travels. The Justice Department, acting under a new law, is preparing to distribute to all police, prosecutors and courts the names of all persons charged anywhere with drug offenses. In addition, the Justice Department keeps the names of more than 13,000 persons who have urged violence or had a connection with riots. The Department of Transportation has the name and offense record of 2.6 million persons in all the states who have had a driver's license suspended or revoked.

The ACLU is not alone in its concern about all these data banks. Their growth has deeply alarmed Senator Sam Ervin, who heads the Senate Sub-Committee on Constitutional Rights. In 1970, Senator Ervin warned the nation against the "vast network of intelligence-oriented systems which are being developed willy-nilly throughout our land, by government and private industries."

He added further, "I believe that in these systems, where they contain the record of the individual's thoughts, beliefs, habits, attitudes and personal activities, there may well rest a potential for political control and for intimidation which is alien to a society of free men."

The American Civil Liberties Union has been working closely with Senator Ervin and his committee in an attempt to place effective controls on all data bank operations, and to give citizens the right to examine and challenge information that may harm their reputations or their ability to get jobs.

As Lawrence Speiser, former director of the ACLU's Washington office, said in arguing against a proposed Federal Data Center in 1967, "Once an unreliable bit of information makes its way into a file, it forms an indelible mark on that person's record. The individual denied employment or some other opportunity on the basis of such information is given no chance to rebut or disprove it. There would be no escape. No mistakes would ever be undone. Skeletons in the closet would always be there, only they would be compactly and efficiently transformed into eternal electrical impulses on tape."

Nevertheless, the government is moving ahead with its plans for a broader program of surveillance, aimed especially at militant left-wing groups and individuals. Local police forces around the country have been getting federal aid to help them build up advanced surveillance systems. Oklahoma set up secret data files on some 6,000 people who were considered actual or potential troublemakers. For this project, the state received a federal grant of $18,347 in 1970, specifying that the money would be used for "surveillance of potential dissident activities." The dossiers were kept by the state's Office of Inter-Agency Coordination.

In October 1970, the ACLU and its Oklahoma affiliate launched a suit to have the agency disbanded and its secret files destroyed. The ACLU charged that a number of Oklahomans had been "blacklisted" as a result of these dossiers. For example, several blacks and whites who had taken part in peace rallies or racial demonstrations had begun having trouble finding jobs or getting into college. One young man who helped edit a controversial underground newspaper was rejected as a teacher by 20 school districts even though he had top grades and excellent references.

However, Oklahoma Governor Dewey F. Bartlett denied that the agency kept a blacklist, and said that the dossiers were available only to qualified police agencies for "intelligence purposes." They enabled the police to make advance plans to prevent civil disorder, Governor Bartlett said.

Of those listed in the dossiers, only about 2,000 were residents of Oklahoma. The rest were "known troublemakers" from other states.

The ACLU suit charged that the purpose of the agency and its dossiers was to "harass and intimidate." This type of secret data storage casts "a pall over lawful political protests in the state of Oklahoma" and deters dissidents from exercising their

First Amendment rights. The ACLU also said that the dossiers created a climate of fear that the information "will be released to numerous Federal and state agencies and to private employers on request."

Because of this pressure from the ACLU, as well as other groups, Oklahoma eventually dropped its surveillance program.

Aside from the growth of data banks, the government had broadened its surveillance of citizens by the increasing use of police spies. According to the ACLU, more and more undercover agents have been infiltrating radical and anti-war groups to gather information on their activities. These agents also attend lawful public rallies for the purpose of photographing the participants, jotting down license numbers of cars that are parked nearby and collecting whatever other data they can.

In the face of this growing threat to lawful assembly, the ACLU adopted a new policy in 1970 opposing the use of undercover agents in private associations because they endanger the rights of speech, association and privacy.

In announcing its new policy, the ACLU pointed out that police agents have been used historically by governments to "discourage or crush opposition to official policies." The Union declared that "citizens have the right to associate among themselves to achieve social or political objectives . . . without interference by the government. The introduction of government spies facilitates the collection of information which is none of the government's business."

The ACLU also charged that when people know that police spies have been infiltrating controversial groups, it makes them afraid to join. Furthermore, the Union declared that spies often encourage illegal acts in order to publicly discredit the group and "entrap members in criminal acts."

To halt this type of undercover activity, the ACLU has filed lawsuits in a number of cases across the country. In New Orleans, La., the Union is challenging the police practice of filming all public events where "controversial" views are expressed. A New York suit was filed on behalf of persons who gathered in Union Square, Manhattan, to board buses that would take them to a demonstration for the Black Panthers in New Haven, Conn. The New York police used audio-visual equipment to record the activities in the Square. Another suit was directed against the Richmond, Va., police, who routinely photographed lawful public meetings and rallies.

In Los Angeles, the ACLU sued to halt the collection of political dossiers by the Los Angeles Police Department. The Union claimed that the police were keeping intelligence files on church, political, educational and social welfare organizations and on persons associated with these groups. Much of the information was obtained through the use of spies, the ACLU charged. A similar suit was filed in New Jersey.

In a letter to all its affiliates in 1970, the ACLU urged them to look into the matter of police infiltration of political groups in their areas. The ACLU suggested that the affiliates begin by checking police budgets to see if there were any expenditures for special surveillance equipment. Also, all racial and political organizations were urged to report any signs of police surveillance to their local ACLU chapters.

Perhaps even more alarming than the growing use of police undercover agents was the disclosure that the military, too, has been spying on American citizens, including some highly respected political figures.

On December 16, 1970, Senator Sam Ervin charged that

Army Intelligence agents had spied on Senator Adlai E. Stevenson, 3rd, former Governor Otto Kerner of Illinois and Representative Abner J. Mikva—all Democrats—as well as on about 800 other civilians in Illinois alone.

Senator Ervin said his information came from a former Army agent who was assigned to political surveillance in Illinois. "The Army investigated these men during their campaigns for office and while they were in office," Senator Ervin charged.

He declared that the military did not limit its investigations to civilians who engaged in violence or other illegal activities. "It was enough," he said, "that they opposed or did not actively support the government's policy in Vietnam or that they disagreed with domestic policies of the Administration, or that they were in contact or sympathetic to people with such views."

Army Secretary Stanley R. Resor strongly denied that the Army had spied on the politicians, although he did not mention the other 800 people. Nevertheless, President Nixon announced that he "totally, completely and unequivocally" objected to military spying on civilian political figures and would not tolerate it during his administration. Congress undertook an investigation of the matter, and the national spotlight was turned on the Army's intelligence activities.

Although Senator Ervin's charges shocked the nation, they were not much of a surprise to the American Civil Liberties Union. Seven months earlier, the ACLU had filed a suit to force the Army to dismantle its civilian intelligence network and destroy the dossiers it had accumulated. The ACLU charged that the Army was keeping computer and microfilm data banks on civilian political activity, and that it had 1,000 plainclothes intelligence agents stationed throughout the country.

Ostensibly, the purpose of the military surveillance system

was to enable the Army to function effectively in case it was needed to help put down domestic disorders.

The ACLU filed suit on the grounds that the Army had no right to collect data on *lawful* political activity since such information could not serve any legitimate military purpose. As Senator Ervin stated: "The business of the Army . . . is to know about the conditions of highways, bridges and facilities. It is not to predict trends and reactions by keeping track of the thoughts and actions of Americans expressing First Amendment freedoms. . . . Regardless of the imagined military objective, the chief casualty of this overkill is the Constitution of the United States, which every military officer and every appointed official has taken an oath to defend."

As more information about the Army's intelligence activities came to light, it was learned from television and newspaper investigations that plainclothes army agents had been circulating at the Republican and Democratic nominating conventions of 1968. They photographed all those present with hidden cameras, used concealed walkie-talkies and had complete files on people who might cause trouble. At the Republican convention in Florida, army agents were housed on board a ship that was docked near the convention site.

During the Democratic convention in Chicago, 7,500 combat troops were on stand-by alert in case of trouble. Army agents were everywhere. They took video tape films of the pitched battle between Chicago police and anti-war demonstrators, and closely watched Senator Eugene McCarthy and his anti-war followers. In fact, army agents monitored a telephone call from McCarthy headquarters to a "known left-wing group," in which McCarthy offered medical help and supplies to those who had been beaten in the melee with the Chicago police.

Army agents also circulated among the protestors at President Nixon's inauguration. The plainclothesmen were supposed to make social contact with the dissenters, and were given money to buy liquor or marijuana, if necessary, to help them establish friendly relations. All this was for the purpose of gathering information and adding more names to the Army's list of potential troublemakers.

Army undercover agents also covered every step of the funeral procession for Martin Luther King, Jr., in 1968, in anticipation of a riot that never occurred. Agents reported on all the dignitaries and personalities who attended the funeral, and they marched all the way with the procession.

Furthermore, when the Poor People's Campaign entered Washington, D. C. in 1968 and set up tents in Resurrection City to protest poverty in America, Army intelligence agents were right there with them, dressed in faded bluejeans and sweatshirts.

The Army first began to expand its domestic spying activities in the mid-1960s, when the first of a long series of urban race riots broke out. The explanation was that the Army might have to come in to put down the riots, so it wanted to be well prepared. At the same time, domestic opposition to the Vietnam War was beginning to mount, so the Army focused its attention on anti-war protestors as well as racial militants.

According to most sources, domestic spying by the Army reached its peak in 1968, and has been on the wane ever since. However, the Army still maintains its dossiers, reports and files on civilian activity in its data banks, and can expand its intelligence apparatus whenever it wishes—as it apparently did in Illinois during the 1970 political campaign.

Shortly after the ACLU filed suit to make the Army disband

its civilian intelligence network, the Army announced that it would stop its surveillance of civilian groups. However, the ACLU was not satisfied with these reassurances, and asked the court for an immediate injunction against the Army.

The ACLU argued that in a democratic society, the people are supposed to keep the government in check. "Any governmental action which reverses these roles—which sees the government monitoring the citizenry . . . poses a grave danger to the very premise which differentiates our nation from the monarchy, autocracy or dictatorship. . . . The intelligence system maintained by the [Army] bears even closer scrutiny by the courts because it is the product of the military arm of government. Our system regards the continued supremacy of the civilian authorities over the military as crucial to survival. The Declaration of Independence contained the following complaint against King George III: 'He has affected to render the military independent and superior to the civil power.' . . ."

The ACLU declared that army surveillance systems were a menace to democracy because "They not only inhibit the freedom of expression protected by the First Amendment, they also infringe upon the privacy of the citizen to pursue his life and beliefs free of governmental interference or direction."

The idea that personal information about many thousands of Americans is being filed away by the government in electronic data banks is repugnant to a free society. Yet this has been the price of our technological advancement. Before the days of computers and microfilms, there were natural limitations on the amount of material that could be collected and stored by government intelligence agencies. They could not possibly keep a close check on the activities of thousands of basically law-abiding citizens who might be opposing government policies or participating in public rallies and demonstrations. But now that technology has made close surveillance possible, it is happening. Although the ACLU is waging a vigorous campaign to halt the growth of data banks, the success of its efforts remains to be seen.

The government is not the only culprit in this matter. Many private organizations, too, have been amassing personal information on people, although for entirely different reasons. Foremost among these groups are the credit bureaus.

Nowadays, almost all Americans have to rely on their personal credit from time to time. If a man wants to finance a house or a car, or open a charge account in a department store, or buy a major appliance on installments, or get a home improvement loan or rent an apartment, he has to show that he is a good credit risk—meaning that he will be likely to make his payments promptly and fully. This is where the credit bureaus come in.

Credit bureaus keep files on millions of individuals, with information about their jobs, salaries, spending habits, financial assets, etc. When a store, a bank or a landlord wants to know if a man is a good credit risk, they don't have to investigate him themselves; they can ask a credit bureau to do the investigating for them. The bureau then issues a report based on its findings. In this way, the credit bureaus amass files on millions of people who, at one time or another, have applied for credit.

In 1967, consumer credit in the United States reached $95 billion, aside from home mortgages. The "buy now, pay later" philosophy was sweeping the country, and 60 percent of the average American's income was devoted to paying off credit obligations.

The growth of credit bureaus has gone hand in hand with

the spectacular growth of credit itself. In 1906, the first credit group in the country, The Associated Credit Bureaus of America, was formed. It had 25 members. Today, this organization has more than 2,200 member bureaus, servicing 400,000 credit grantors—and it keeps credit files on more than 110 million individuals. In 1967, this group issued 97.1 million reports.

A typical credit file on an individual would include items of personal identification, employment history, personal history, public records (such as arrests, law suits filed, judgments, marriages, divorces, bankruptcies, etc.) and credit history (size of accounts, defaults, etc.). Sometimes, credit bureaus get their information by interviewing an individual's employer, landlord, neighbors, fellow workers or banker.

The existence of these credit bureau dossiers on millions of individuals poses two major problems: (1) Are the files accurate? (2) Are the files being used in ways that intrude on people's right to privacy?

Unfortunately, there have been many stories about people who suddenly found they could not obtain credit, even though they had a good income and had always paid their debts on time. A credit bureau may have listed them as a "poor risk" for some reason, and the hapless individuals were not even able to find out why. In most cases, credit bureaus do not allow individuals to see their own dossiers, so mistakes often go uncorrected.

The ACLU strongly urged Congress to place some controls on credit bureaus so that such injustices could be held to a minimum. The ACLU felt that individuals should have three basic protections: first, they must have the right to inspect their files; second, they must have the right to contest the accuracy of the information; and third, they must have the right to place in their files their own explanation of any unsatisfactory financial behavior. This last point is most important, because sometimes a credit bureau will brand a person as a "slow payer" without adding the reason for his delay in paying, such as prolonged illness or temporary unemployment. These protections would go a long way towards halting the spread of erroneous or misleading information about people, and should not be too difficult to put into practice.

However, the matter of guaranteeing people's right of privacy is more difficult. Ostensibly, credit bureaus are not supposed to release personal information about people to anybody other than credit grantors. But it is well known that these dossiers can be obtained very easily by unauthorized persons, such as federal investigators and police agents. In fact, the Associated Credit Bureaus of America freely—and proudly—admits this. In one of its publications, the group stated: "The Washington and regional offices of the Federal Bureau of Investigation are among the largest users of credit bureau services. FBI agents are constantly checking ACB of A credit bureaus' records for information to use in connection with their investigations."

Apparently, private parties can also get this information without any difficulty. To test this suspicion, Professor Alan Westin, former chairman of the Privacy Committee of the ACLU, tried an experiment.

In his private capacity, Dr. Westin is Professor of Public Law and Government at Columbia University. One day in February 1968, he had a member of his staff at Columbia write a letter to the Greater New York Credit Bureau asking for a report on the "character" of a female research assistant who, he said, was being considered for a promotion at the University. (The research assistant had agreed to the use of her name in this experiment.)

In testifying about this experiment before the House Sub-Committee on Invasion of Privacy, Dr. Westin said: "We had no credit purpose and offered none. . . . The letter must have arrived at the Credit Bureau in the morning mail of the 21st. At 10 AM on that same day, the Executive Manager telephoned and read us a full 'Previous Residence Report' on the employee in question, containing information about her residence, employment and credit history in another city before she came to New York, and similar information since her arrival in New York City. This included entries for questions about her 'character, habits and morals,' how she was regarded by her employer, whether there was any 'indication of illegal practices past or present,' and 'suits, judgments or bankruptcies,' her estimated monthly income, 'other income' from rentals, investments, etc., and a considerable list of other items. There was no check made to see whether this girl really was an employee at our Center or whether she wished this 'credit' information to be revealed."

Continuing his testimony, Dr. Westin said, "All of this was done, incidentally, without charge to us, 'as a courtesy,' the manager indicated, even though we offered to pay the customary fees. This may have been intended as a gesture of goodwill towards a University Center, but it was an outrageous disclosure of personal information and a breach of this woman's privacy. If I could obtain a credit report this easily, I cannot help wondering whether there is any security and confidentiality for personal information held in the Greater New York Credit Bureau. And, one must ask, is this Bureau—with its 8.5 million individual files, 3 million annual reports and 500 employees—typical of many others throughout the nation?"

Because of such disclosures, the ACLU strongly backed the

Federal Fair Credit Reporting Act, passed in April 1970, which restricted the credit bureau's freedom to give out personal information.

Although the ACLU does not feel that the credit bureaus should abandon the use of computers and data banks, it does feel that the people are entitled to greater protection. As the ACLU says, "The complexity of our existence requires this reliance on these mechanized information systems in order to cope with the highly involved decision-making process which our society demands. However, unless we are going to sacrifice the constitutionally protected liberty of the citizen as a price for the benefits brought by computers, we must build in protections now so that the liberties of individual citizens are not ignored as our reliance upon these machines grows. Computers themselves will not perform this task for us."

[7]
THE RIGHT TO EAT

During the 1960s, the ACLU came to realize that there were large groups of people in America who were hardly being protected by the Bill of Rights at all. For them, the Bill of Rights might just as well not have existed. These "disinherited" people included welfare recipients, the mentally ill, migrant workers, prisoners, soldiers and students.

To help them, the ACLU set up the Roger Baldwin Foundation in 1967. This was done mainly for financial reasons. If the ACLU wanted to expand its activities and wage a large-scale legal campaign to aid the "disinherited," it needed a great deal more money. The Roger Baldwin Foundation was formed as a tax-exempt arm of the ACLU that would try to attract foundation grants and other large contributions. With these funds, it would sponsor major legal, research and educational projects in specific areas.

During the first year it was created, the Foundation received about $200,000 in grants to begin its projects. Since then, contributions have grown to about $750,000 annually, enabling the new branch to greatly expand its projects. In 1970, the name of the group was changed to the American Civil Liberties Foundation in order to avoid confusing people who didn't realize that the Foundation was part of the ACLU.

When the Foundation was formed in 1967, the ACLU appointed a 33-year-old trial lawyer from New York, Martin Garbus, as executive director. At that time, Mr. Garbus was already working on a very significant welfare case that he took with him when he changed jobs. It became the Foundation's first major case in the drive to aid the "disinherited," and resulted in a stunning victory—one that affected more than 400,000 needy children.

The case revolved around Mrs. Sylvester Smith, a 34-year-old black woman who lived in Alabama. Mrs. Smith, who had been widowed once and deserted once, was the mother of four children. She worked as a cook, but earned only about $20 a week. To supplement this meager income, she had been getting welfare money for her family under the Aid to Dependent Children Program.

The ADC program was designed to help children who have lost a parent by death, incapacity or "continued absence from the home." Most of the money for this program comes from the federal government, under the Social Security Act. The remainder is supplied by the states. In Alabama, the federal government supplies 83 percent of the ADC funds, while the state puts up only 17 percent.

The program has been strongly attacked by those who feel it encourages immoral behavior, especially among blacks. In 1959, Arkansas Governor Orval Faubus lashed out against the ADC program, saying, "By taxing the good people to pay for these programs, we are putting a premium on illegitimacy never before known in the world."

In this spirit, the state of Alabama, as well as 18 other states plus the District of Columbia, placed certain restrictions on the federally-aided welfare programs. They were called "substitute father" or "man in the house" rules. That is, if a welfare mother was having sexual relations with a man—even a man who did not live in the house with her—that man was presumed to be a "substitute father" to the woman's children, and responsible for their support. Thus, the state could end welfare payments to the family. The state did not have to show that the man actually was helping to support the children, or that he had the financial means to do so. It only had to show that he was having sexual relations with the mother; that fact alone was enough to disqualify her and her children from the welfare program.

Alabama passed a "substitute father" rule in June 1964. During the next few years, the state dropped about 18,000 children from the welfare rolls. Almost all of them were black, so the result was that Alabama had shaved its welfare costs at the expense of poor black families.

Mrs. Smith was one of the welfare mothers who had been hurt by Alabama's "substitute father" rule. She had been receiving about $29 a month in welfare payments, which was more than one-quarter of her entire family income. Even so, the total was less than the established level of "need" for a family that size. In an article in *The New York Times Magazine,* August 25, 1968, Walter Goodman wrote of Mrs. Smith's history and her struggle to continue to get aid for her children.

She had first applied for welfare in March 1956, a few months after her husband was killed "in a fight over a woman." At that time she lived in Tyler, Alabama, was 23 years old and had three children: Ida Elizabeth, 3; Ernestine, 2; and Willie Lewis, 6 months. Her children met all the requirements for financial aid under the ADC program, so help was granted.

In 1957, Mrs. Smith had a fourth child by a man named Louis Fuller. Mr. Fuller lived with Mrs. Smith for several years, but deserted her in June 1963. His child then became eligible for the ADC program, so that Mrs. Smith was receiving a total of about $67 in welfare aid for her children. However, in March 1966, Mrs. Smith's daughter, Ida Elizabeth, 13 years old and unmarried, bore a child of her own, so she was taken off the ADC lists.

That same year, Mrs. Smith moved to Selma, Ala., where she had found a job as a cook and waitress in a café. She worked from 3:30 AM to noon for $16 a week. Later her salary was raised to $20. Because of this income, Mrs. Smith's welfare payments were reduced.

After Mrs. Smith moved to Selma, a new caseworker named Jacquelyn Stancil was assigned to the Smith family. In going through the records, Mrs. Stancil came across the name of a man, William E. Williams, who was listed as a good friend of Mrs. Smith. Her suspicions aroused, Mrs. Stancil questioned several people and learned that Mrs. Smith was receiving weekend visits from Mr. Williams, who lived 15 miles away in Tyler.

In September 1966, Mrs. Stancil told Mrs. Smith that her aid would be stopped if she continued to see Mr. Williams. Despite the fact that Mr. Williams was married and had nine children of his own, and couldn't possibly support the Smith children, too, he was considered a "substitute father" under Alabama law.

Mrs. Smith was furious, and flatly refused to promise that she would end her affair with Mr. Williams. "If God had intended for me to be a nun I'd be a nun," she said.

Aid for the Smith children was discontinued. This meant that the family of six—Mrs. Smith, her four children and her grandchild—had to try to survive on Mrs. Smith's $20-a-week paycheck.

Outraged by these events, Mrs. Smith felt it was unjust for the welfare people to punish her family—which she had kept together for years by hard work and determination—just because they didn't like her private activities. She took her story to some civil rights workers in Selma, and they put her in touch with the Center on Social Welfare Policy, which had been set up at Columbia University to handle cases for welfare clients. Martin Garbus was co-director of the Center, and he and the other attorneys there decided to take Mrs. Smith's case.

"The facts were perfect," Mr. Garbus said. "If Alabama had any sense, they would have restored Mrs. Smith's aid and tried to wash out the action. The so-called substitute father was not in fact the father of any of the children; he was not living in their home or performing any of a father's duties; he was under no obligation to contribute to their support, and in fact he was not contributing."

The Smith case was a clear example of a state denying aid to desperately poor children as punishment for the sexual behavior of their mother.

Although Reuben King, commissioner of Alabama's department of Pensions and Security, denied that this was Alabama's way of discouraging immoral behavior, he said that any mother whose aid was stopped could always choose "to give up her pleasure or to act like a woman ought to act like and continue to receive aid."

When Mr. Garbus left the Center on Social Welfare Policy to go to the ACLU Foundation, he took Mrs. Smith's case with him. In November 1966, he began the legal proceedings that wound up in the Supreme Court two years later. This was the first welfare case ever argued before the Supreme Court.

Mr. Garbus based the case against Alabama on several grounds. First, he said that although the state was not required by the Constitution to aid the needy, once it did set up a welfare program, it had to abide by the equal protection guarantees of the Constitution. That is, as long as the children met the state's definition of dependent children, Alabama could not "pick and choose the mothers and children it will aid in a whimsical or capricious manner."

Furthermore, he charged, the real purpose of the substitute father rule was to deny benefits to blacks. About 95 percent of the persons affected by the rule were blacks, and Mr. Garbus said that state officials knew this would be the case when they first proposed the rule.

In addition, he said that the rule violated the due process guarantee of the Constitution, since welfare recipients did not even have the right to a hearing before their benefits were canceled. Also, the language of the rule was vague; it called for termination of benefits whenever there "appears" to be a substitute father.

Perhaps worst of all, the rule violated the right to privacy. Mr. Garbus called it an "onerous" law because it meant that a mother who wanted to save her children from starvation had to "come forward, bare the intimacies of her bedroom, and strip herself of all dignity."

The time was right for the Supreme Court to hear its first welfare case. With about 9 million Americans on public welfare in 1967, and the laws in a tangle, something had to be done about abusive and arbitrary welfare rules. The recipients were in no position to help themselves since they depended on the welfare system for the food they ate and the clothes they wore. They couldn't afford private lawyers to handle their complaints, so it was up to civil rights groups like the ACLU to take up the fight for them. The Supreme Court, which was so closely identified with civil rights under Chief Justice Earl Warren, seemed ready to move from school and voting cases to the new area of welfare rights.

The Right to Eat

The *Smith* case was argued shortly after the assassination of Martin Luther King, Jr., and the atmosphere in the courtroom was tense and emotional. Mr. Garbus argued heatedly that the Alabama rule discriminated against "helpless children" who were being deprived of their "right to life."

In response, Alabama Assistant Attorney General Mary Stapp argued that by cutting off aid to mothers having illicit affairs, Alabama was providing more money for families who lived up to all the standards. This prompted Justice Brennan to note acidly, "You give more milk to some children by giving none to others."

The justices questioned Mrs. Stapp intensively about the circumstances under which poor families could have their aid cut off. When she continually avoided direct answers, Chief Justice Warren ended the hearing by saying, "Never mind! Never mind!" and slamming a book down on his desk.

In June 1968, the Supreme Court struck down Alabama's "substitute father" rule. The Court held that under the Aid to Dependent Children Program, only persons who had a *legal* obligation to support the children—that is, their real fathers or their mother's husbands—could be regarded as parents.

Speaking for a unanimous Court, Chief Justice Warren said that "destitute children who are legally fatherless cannot be flatly denied federally funded assistance on the transparent fiction that they have a substitute father."

He said that under the Social Security Act, aid was to be granted to *all* eligible children, and that the mother's sexual conduct in no way lessened her children's eligibility or their need for help. The Court declared that Alabama was not free to discourage immorality by disqualifying needy children from aid.

Although the Court's decision in the Alabama case would also apply to every other state that had similar "substitute father" or "man in the house" rules, there were signs that some states might not comply with the decision until they, too, were dragged into court.

In Michigan, the director of social services pledged that he would continue denying aid to children whose mothers were having extra-marital affairs. A Republican state representative supported this by saying, "What the Supreme Court has told us, in substance, is that we must subsidize not only illegitimacy but adultery."

Since more than 400,000 needy children have been hurt by these attempts to enforce sexual morality, the ACLU Foundation did not intend to see its victory in the *Smith* case wasted. It pledged to continue the battle to bring reluctant states into line, either by bringing every one of them to court or by forcing the Department of Health, Education and Welfare to withhold funds from states that did not comply with the Supreme Court decision.

The *Smith* case was just the beginning of the ACLU Foundation's drive for a welfare "bill of rights." Believing that people must not be reduced in the eyes of the law because they are poor, the Foundation has attacked other injustices in the welfare system. It opposed the one-year residency requirement for welfare applicants that had been passed by 40 states. In 1969, the Supreme Court declared that these residency requirements were unconstitutional, stating that they infringed on the right of poor people to travel freely from state to state and on the Fourteenth Amendment's guarantee of equal protection of the laws.

The ACLU has also filed suit against New York's welfare rule that forces recipients to pay back all the benefits they have received if and when they have funds. Thirty-two states have such "recovery" programs. The Foundation contends that they prevent people from ever becoming self-supporting, thereby conflicting with the purposes of the Social Security Act.

The ACLU suit was filed on behalf of several New York welfare recipients. The first, Geraldine Snell, was a Brooklyn mother of four who was attending college on a scholarship and working part-time for $32 a week. To be eligible for welfare, she had to sell her assets—which consisted only of the cooperative apartment she had bought for $900 several years earlier—and to turn over the money from this sale to the Welfare Department. She and her family were ordered to move elsewhere. In addition, Mrs. Snell expected to be self-supporting after earning her teaching degree. But under the welfare regulations, she would have to repay all the benefits she got for herself and her children over the years. A debt of this size would keep her in poverty for the forseeable future.

The second welfare recipient involved in the Foundation suit was Miriam Ramos, a 19-year-old mother of three small children whose husband was in jail. When she and her eldest child were injured in an automobile accident, she had to turn over the money received from a personal injury claim to the Welfare Department. Thus, she could not use the money to better her position, but had to remain on welfare.

Juan Malave, the third person involved in the lawsuit, earned $86 a week and was the father of eight children. An injury put him out of work temporarily, and he applied for welfare benefits during this period. When he was back on his feet and working again, the Welfare Department billed him $420.29 to cover the benefits it had paid him. At this salary, it was a terrible hardship to repay a debt of that size—a debt undertaken out of the necessity to eat.

The ACLU Foundation pointed out that in each of these cases, poor people had to repay the state for the cash benefits they had received. But wealthier people also receive benefits from the government, such as oil depletion allowances, farm subsidies and transportation subsidies, and they *never* have to repay these benefits. This, said the Foundation, was a denial of the equal protection of the laws.

Furthermore, the Foundation said, the purpose of the Social Security Act was to "help maintain and strengthen family life," and to aid adults in becoming self-supporting and independent. Social work experts have testified that when very poor people know they have to repay all the money they are receiving for the bare necessities of life, it depresses their ambition and increases their sense of dependency. Thus, the "recovery" law conflicts with the purposes and intent of the Social Security Act.

Although the ACLU Foundation felt that this was one of its most important cases in establishing a welfare "bill of rights" and helping people get off welfare, the Supreme Court declined to hear it. Thus, a lower court decision upholding New York's welfare "recovery" law still stands.

However, in other welfare cases, the ACLU Foundation was far more successful. The Foundation had launched an all-out attack on what it considered the most tragic abuses of the welfare system—the practice in many states of cutting off aid to welfare recipients without giving them a hearing first. Over the years, about three million welfare clients had been dropped from the relief rolls throughout the nation without a prior hearing.

By 1970, the ACLU Foundation had brought two cases of this type to the Supreme Court, one involving the state of California, the other involving New York. In arguing these cases, the ACLU cited many examples of what happens when welfare payments are cut off without warning and without any sort of advance hearing.

There was one instance where a woman with four children had to live on handouts because her payments stopped suddenly, and for no apparent reason. One day she and her children ate some spoiled food they had found, and all five of them landed in the hospital with food poisoning. Later, she went to her local welfare center for emergency aid, where they kept her waiting eight hours. After she fainted, they gave her $15 to feed herself and her children.

Another example of welfare injustice also involved a woman with four young children. When her welfare checks stopped coming, she could not pay her rent. She and her children moved in with a sister who had nine children and was also on welfare. This meant that 13 children and two adults were jammed into one small apartment. Months later, after the woman kept protesting to the Welfare Department, the officials finally realized they had made a mistake. The woman was fully eligible for welfare, and her payments never should have stopped in the first place.

The ACLU charged that none of these injustices would have occurred if the recipients had been given a hearing *before* their payments were stopped, instead of after.

The Supreme Court agreed. Speaking for the majority, Justice Brennan said that cutting off welfare payments without a prior hearing was a denial of the "due process of law" clause of the Fourteenth Amendment. The most vital requirement of the "due process" clause, he said, is the opportunity to be heard before punishment is meted out. Otherwise, in a welfare case, the recipient is deprived of the "very means by which to live while he waits" for redress.

The right to a fair hearing included the right to be represented by a lawyer; to confront and cross-examine unfriendly witnesses; to have a written copy of the decision with a statement of the reasons based solely on evidence examined at the hearing; and to have an impartial decision maker.

On the heels of this victory, the ACLU Foundation helped win another welfare case in the Supreme Court, *Rosado vs. Wyman.* The ACLU did not handle this case directly, but filed a friend-of-the-court brief on behalf of more than a dozen organizations.

The case concerned New York State's attempt in 1969 to cut welfare payments to 66¢ a day per person for all food and personal needs, despite a sharp rise in the cost of living.

According to the regulations of the Department of Health, Education and Welfare, each state must set up a realistic standard of need based on the cost of living within the state. This standard has to be changed periodically to reflect changes in the cost of living. Thus, if the cost of living in a particular state goes up, that state must raise its standard of need accordingly.

However, there is a loophole in this law. A state does not have to pay welfare clients the *full* standard of need if it feels it cannot afford to. Poorer states, like Mississippi, pay only a percentage of the standard of need. New York, however, traditionally paid 100 percent of need.

In 1969, New York wanted to cut its welfare costs, but without the embarrassment of admitting that it could not pay 100 percent of need. So instead of doing this, the legislature simply reduced the *standard* of need to 66¢ per day, and continued to pay 100 percent of it. However, this change violated the federal requirement that a state's standard of need must reflect cost-of-living changes. In New York, the cost of living had gone up about 7 percent during 1969, so it could not legitimately reduce the standard of need in the face of rising costs.

A New York welfare recipient, Julia Rosado, challenged New York's action, and the case reached the Supreme Court a year later. The Court ruled against New York, declaring that: (1) a state must set a *realistic* standard of need based on the cost of subsistence living in the state; and (2) a state must declare what percentage of need its welfare payments are meant to cover.

Although the *Rosado* case was a legal victory for the poor, in practice it didn't actually help them very much. New York was still determined to keep its welfare costs down, so even though it had to raise its standard of need, it simply said that it could not afford to pay 100 percent of its own standard anymore.

This is an example of the difficulties the ACLU Foundation is facing in trying to help welfare recipients. Nevertheless, since the ACLU brought the first welfare case to the Supreme Court in 1968, the Court has begun to lay down a body of uniform rules affecting the welfare systems of the 50 states. This should eventually bring to an end the whimsical and unjust ways in which states sometimes treat welfare clients. However, there is still much to be done. The ACLU also wants to establish more respect for welfare recipients' right of privacy, and to bring an end to frequent searches and inspections of welfare homes, intrusive questioning and requests for self-incriminating answers. Welfare clients often don't object to these actions, the ACLU points out, because they're afraid of losing their benefits.

Among the other "disinherited" groups the ACLU Foundation has been trying to protect are migrant workers, particularly in California. At the time the ACLU Foundation was set up in 1967, these poverty-stricken workers were not protected by the National Labor Act or by any existing legal institutions, and were almost wholly at the mercy of the growers who hired them. Cesar Chavez was trying to organize these migrants into a union, but they were so downtrodden, and the growers put up such resistance, that the job was terribly difficult. When the union tried to call a strike, the growers recruited strike-breakers from Texas and Mexico.

One of the first tasks the ACLU Foundation set for itself was to protect the migrant workers' right to speak freely, distribute literature and picket. This was an old-fashioned battle for the rights of labor, similar to thousands that the ACLU had fought in the 1930s; but now it was the 1960s and the migrant workers stood out as one of the few unorganized labor groups left in America. Most other workers had prospered over the years with the help of their unions, but for the migrants, the Depression had never ended.

Cesar Chavez, head of the United Farm Workers Organizing Committee of the AFL–CIO, was a charismatic labor leader who was having some success in rallying the migrants. One of the great difficulties, however, was that the migrants were so hard to reach. During the growing season, they lived and worked in labor camps on the growers' property, where union organizers could not get near them. When the growing season was over, the migrants scattered all over so that it was impossible to organize them.

Mr. Chavez and his fellow workers had tried to get around this problem by setting up amplifying systems outside the labor camps to speak to the migrants while they were working in the fields. It was the only way they could talk to the workers about the benefits of joining the union while they were all together.

However, one grower, the Giumarra Brothers Fruit Company, got an injunction against Cesar Chavez and his group to prevent them from "using any mechanical device for the purpose of amplifying one's voice and directing the same towards employees while [these employees] are engaged in their work."

The United Farm Workers, backed by the ACLU Foundation, fought the injunction on the grounds that they were being deprived of "their right to freedom of speech for that period during which that right is most vital to them, the growing season. To take away [the union's] right to speak to the workers is to take away their only weapon."

The labor union eventually succeeded in organizing a boycott against Giumarra Brothers and other California grape growers, forcing them to recognize the union as a bargaining agent for the migrants.

Another early ACLU lawsuit on behalf of the migrant workers took place in Texas. The ACLU charged that Texas Rangers had beaten and pistol-whipped UFWOC organizers on picket lines and in their homes. In addition, the ACLU said there was a conspiracy between the Rangers, Texas melon farmers, county officials and state courts to deny the civil rights of UFWOC members.

Migrant workers and welfare clients are just two of the disadvantaged groups whose rights have been neglected for so long. The ACLU Foundation is rapidly expanding its activities on their behalf, and is hoping to establish a new "bill of rights for the disinherited."

[8]
A BILL OF RIGHTS FOR THE YOUNG

The great majority of America's youth are well fed, warmly clothed and generally well cared for. They hardly seem like a "disinherited" group to most people, but the ACLU sees them in a different light. That is, the Union believes that young people have not been getting the full protection of the Bill of Rights, even though they are entitled to it as well as adults.

To challenge the nation's legal treatment of its young, the ACLU brought a very significant case to the Supreme Court in 1967 on behalf of Gerald Gault, who had been judged a juvenile delinquent three years earlier when he was 15. The boy had been sent to the Arizona Industrial School for having made "lewd telephone calls."

The case was a shocking miscarriage of justice for several reasons. Neither the boy nor his parents had been notified of the charges against him. He was not given the right to counsel or the right to confront and cross-examine witnesses. He was never told of his right against self-incrimination, and he did not have the right of appeal.

As outrageous as these facts may seem, they were not unusual. At that time, juvenile courts did not operate according to the same standards as adult courts. In the firm belief that they should, the ACLU took the *Gault* case up to the Supreme

Court in the hope of winning the same constitutional protections for young people that adults enjoyed.

On May 15, 1967, the Supreme Court handed down a landmark decision in the *Gault* case. The Court held that children, as well as adults, were entitled to the basic due process protections of the Bill of Rights. Speaking for the Court, Justice Abe Fortas said that children had the right to receive timely notice of the charges against them; the right to a lawyer, appointed by the court if necessary, in any case where they faced detention in a juvenile home or reform school; the right to confront and cross-examine hostile witnesses; and the right to remain silent to avoid self-incrimination.

"Under our Constitution," the Court stated, "the condition of being a boy does not justify a kangaroo court. If Gerald had been over 18, he would not have been subject to juvenile court proceedings. For the particular offense immediately involved, the maximum punishment would have been a fine of $5 to $50, or imprisonment in jail for not more than two months. Instead, he was committed to custody for a maximum of six years."

The Court deplored the "wide gulf between the state's treatment of the adult and of the child," and said that the gap had to be narrowed.

As a result of this decision, radical changes were made in most of the nation's 3,000 juvenile courts, so that children would no longer have their rights trampled upon.

The *Gault* case marked the start of a series of cases involving the legal rights of children. Many of them centered on the treatment of children in the schools, where youngsters had no recourse against the many rules and regulations set down by school officials. Even though these rules sometimes violated the Bill of Rights, it was thought that constitutional guarantees did not

A Bill of Rights for the Young

apply to children in a classroom setting. However, the ACLU thought differently, and set about to extend these guarantees to students, whether in college, high school or, in some cases, elementary school.

One of the most important cases of this type began early on the morning of December 16, 1965, when 13-year-old Mary Beth Tinker left her house in Des Moines, Iowa, wearing a piece of black ribbon tied around her arm. The arm band meant that Mary Beth was mourning all those who had died in the Vietnam War, and that she wanted a Christmas truce that would last indefinitely. The holiday truce had been suggested first by Robert Kennedy, and many Americans were donning the arm bands to show their support for this proposal.

As Mary Beth headed towards Warren Harding Junior High School that morning, she was somewhat nervous. School officials in Des Moines had passed a rule forbidding arm bands in the schools after they learned that many students planned to wear them in class. But Mary Beth and several others decided to wear them anyhow, because they felt the issue was so important. Mary Beth was a Quaker, and even at her young age she had already been involved in anti-war protests and civil rights demonstrations.

When she arrived in school, her friends noticed her arm band immediately, and some urged her to take it off for fear she would get into trouble. Her teachers, however, did not seem to notice, and the morning passed uneventfully.

But in the afternoon, Mary Beth was called down to the office of the girls' adviser, Mrs. Vera Ann Tarmann. As Mary Beth testified later, Mrs. Tarmann "told me she was sorry she had to do it, because she understood my point of view because her grandparents had been Quakers, or something like that, and then she told me she would have to suspend me. She said that she had to follow orders, but she sympathized with my opinion."

At that point, Mary Beth Tinker was officially suspended from Warren Harding Junior High School—marking the opening round in a battle that would eventually go all the way up to the Supreme Court. At stake was this basic question: Do First Amendment guarantees of free speech give students the right to wear symbols of political views to school?

Mary Beth Tinker was not the only student involved in the case. Her 15-year-old brother, John, had been sent home from North High School and told not to come back until he had removed his arm band. A third student, Christopher Eckhardt, 15, was sent home from Roosevelt High School for the same offense. However, in Christopher's case, school officials applied greater pressure on him to remove the arm band, apparently out of fear that the incident would create bad publicity for the school.

As Christopher testified later, the school's vice principal "had told me that I had a good record with the school and asked me if I was looking for a busted nose, and I told him that I wasn't, and he said something to the effect that that is what it was going to look like on my record for being suspended from school, and Mrs. Cross [girls' adviser] informed me that the colleges didn't accept demonstrators or protestors. . . ."

Although the students returned to their schools without arm bands after the Christmas vacation, they and their parents did not let the matter drop. With the support of the American Civil Liberties Union, they began the long series of hearings and appeals that finally reached the Supreme Court four years later in *Tinker vs. Des Moines, Iowa, School Board*.

School officials had been claiming that they could outlaw

arm bands and other political symbols as part of their right to keep order and regulate conduct in the classrooms. They pointed out that the Vietnam War was a highly inflammatory issue in 1965, and the wearing of anti-war symbols by a few students might have provoked fights or arguments, creating an atmosphere in which learning was impossible.

The ACLU, on the other hand, said that the wearing of political symbols was a form of speech that was protected by the Constitution, and that such a right was "lifeless" if it was not encouraged during school years. Students must be allowed to practice civil liberties, as well as study about them, the ACLU said.

The Supreme Court agreed. On February 24, 1969, the Court stated in the *Tinker* case that neither students nor teachers "shed their constitutional rights to freedom of expression at the schoolhouse gate." The Court went on to declare that "in our system state-operated schools may not be enclaves of totalitarianism. School officials do not possess absolute authority over their students. Students in school as well as out are 'persons' under our Constitution. They are possessed of fundamental rights which the state must respect, just as they themselves must respect their obligations to the State. . . ."

The Court pointed out that if the wearing of arm bands had actually touched off disturbances in the schools, it would be a different matter. But officials could not ban the wearing of political symbols *in advance,* simply out of fear that they might cause fights. Such fear is "not enough to overcome the right to freedom of expression. . . . Any variation from the majority's opinion may inspire fear. Any word spoken in class, in the lunchroom or on the campus that deviates from the views of another person may start an argument or cause a disturbance. But our Constitution says we must take this risk. . . ."

The *Tinker* case firmly established that every student has the right to peacefully express his views in the schools, and that this right can't be curtailed at the whim of school officials. As Melvin Wulf, ACLU Legal Director said after the Court announced its opinion, "Student rights to free speech are firmly rooted now, and the wrangling about student papers, political campaigning, picketing and other forms of peaceful expression should come to an end."

But students are demanding other kinds of freedoms as well. They want to be free to wear their hair whatever length they please, to sport a mustache or beard if they choose and to wear the type of clothes they prefer. The American Civil Liberties Union has stood behind students on these issues, too, and is staggering under an especially heavy load of "hair" cases.

During the 1960s, long hair came to represent a type of freedom to many young people—freedom from conformity, freedom from "establishment" values and freedom from the type of world created by the over-30 generations. A boy who let his hair grow long was not just trying out a new style; he was making a personal statement, telling everyone, "This is what I am and what I stand for."

But many high schools and junior high schools across the country had codes regulating the type of clothes and hair styles that students could wear. These codes stemmed from the idea that school officials *must* outlaw odd styles in order to uphold discipline in the classrooms. Long hair on boys was definitely considered odd by many school boards, and growing numbers of students were suspended or expelled for refusing to cut their hair.

Among the earlier cases of this type was one involving a group of three young musicians. In September 1966, Phillip Ferrell, Stephen Webb and Paul Jarvis were not allowed to enroll at W. W. Samuell High School in Dallas, Tex., because they were wearing Beatle-type haircuts. The boys were members of a rock 'n' roll group, "Sounds Unlimited," and according to their contract with their business manager, they had to wear their hair long.

Actually, their hair was not very long compared to the flowing tresses that boys started wearing just a short time later, but it was considered long in 1966. Stephen Webb's hair, as described in testimony by his mother, was "over his ears, but one can see the lobe of his ear. It is not over his collar, but is over his forehead and down to his eyebrows." Phillip Ferrell's hair, if hanging straight forward, would have come below his eyebrows. However, it was brushed to the side.

Because of their appearance, the boys were rejected not only by Samuell High School, but by seven other schools as well. This meant that they would not be able to go to school at all unless they violated their contract and cut their hair.

With the full backing of the ACLU, the boys took their case to court. The ACLU argued that students had the right to wear their hair however they pleased as part of the freedom of speech and self-expression guaranteed by the First and Fourteenth Amendments. In addition, the Union said, forcing students to conform to a particular hair style violated the right of privacy that is implied in the Bill of Rights.

But school board officials argued that if a few boys wore their hair long, it was certain to cause many problems. Other students would be distracted from their work and might taunt or harass the long-haired boys. Thus, the rules governing hair styles were needed to keep order in the schools.

The case, *Ferrell vs. Dallas Independent School District,* went as far as the United States Court of Appeals (5th Circuit), which ruled in March 1968 that the school board's hair regulations were valid. The court said that although hair styles were a form of expression, like thought or speech, such rights were not absolute; they could be infringed upon by the state for compelling reasons, such as "maintaining an effective and efficient school system."

As far as the boys' musical career was concerned, the court suggested that they wear wigs.

Although the ACLU lost the *Ferrell* case, there have been similar cases elsewhere in which the courts upheld the right of students to wear their hair long.

For example, in *Richards vs. Thurston* (1970), the U. S. Court of Appeals (1st Circuit), ruled that Robert Richards of Marlboro, Mass., could not be suspended for refusing to cut his shoulder-length hair.

"We conclude that within the commodious concept of liberty, embracing freedoms great and small, is the right to wear one's hair as he wishes," the court declared.

Mustaches, too, have been a cause of controversy. The Oregon Civil Liberties Union handled a case in which an honor student was suspended from classes in his senior year for growing a mustache. The school penalized him for drawing special attention to himself "through this kind of sensationalism."

But the Federal District Court struck down the regulation and said that the student must be readmitted, mustache and all. It also ordered the school to help the youth make up the work he had missed.

In ruling on the case, Judge Robert C. Belloni said, "I really almost as a matter of law can't conceive of any disciplinary problems or disruption in the Klamath School system because a boy wears a mustache. It isn't necessary to achieve discipline to cast every person in school in the same mold. The Supreme Court has made it clear in a whole lot of very recent

A Bill of Rights for the Young [143]

cases that children have constitutional rights as well as adults. In fact, it seems to me that unreasonable and arbitrary rules imposed by those in authority are themselves the causes of disciplinary problems."

As of this writing, the Supreme Court has refused to review any hair cases, so that there is no constitutional ruling that can be applied nationwide. Whether or not a boy can wear long hair in school still depends very much on what state he lives in. In Wisconsin or Massachusetts, the courts will probably uphold his right to long hair; in Texas, the local courts probably won't. It remains for the Supreme Court to decide the matter on a national basis.

Why should an organization like the ACLU be so concerned with a seemingly trivial issue like hair? Because hair has become a symbol—a symbol of individuality and non-conformism that the ACLU believes must be protected in a free society. It is part of the endless battle of the individual against the state.

Spencer Coxe, Executive Director of the Philadelphia branch of the ACLU, pointed out in *Youth* magazine, "It is no accident that repressive societies have often sought to impose modes of dress and hair styles. The most recent example is mainland China, where for years a national uniform has been foisted upon everybody and where more recently the Red Guards have been administering 'pro-Peking' haircuts. The Red Chinese, like the Nazis before them, grasped the profound psychological truth that looking alike promotes thinking alike and acting alike."

Another issue over which students and their schools frequently clash is freedom of the press. Since the ACLU believes that students must be given the widest possible freedom to express their opinions, it has often defended student editors whose writings got them into serious trouble with school officials.

Gary Clinton Dickey, a top student at Troy State College in Alabama, was among the most active students at Troy. Troy State was one of several colleges owned and operated by the state of Alabama. An English major, Gary was editor-in-chief of the Troy State literary magazine, copy editor of the yearbook and, during the 1966–67 school year, an editor of *The Tripolitan,* the student newspaper.

His troubles began in April 1967, when a controversy broke out in another state-owned school, the University of Alabama. The president there, Dr. Frank Rose, had let students put out a special publication called "Emphasis '67: A World in Revolution." This publication carried excerpts from speeches by revolutionaries such as Stokely Carmichael, former head of the Student Non-Violent Coordinating Committee, and Bettina Aptheker, a communist spokesman. It also carried statements by anti-revolutionaries, such as General Earl Wheeler, Chairman of the Joint Chiefs of Staff.

Nevertheless, the Alabama legislature was enraged over this "radical" publication, and criticized Dr. Rose for allowing it to be published. He stood up firmly for academic freedom—and the battle was on.

Over at Troy State, Gary Dickey wanted to print an editorial in *The Tripolitan* supporting Dr. Rose and criticizing the Alabama legislators. But when he showed his editorial to the faculty adviser and to Troy State President, Ralph Adams, they told him he couldn't print it. Instead, the faculty adviser gave Dickey a substitute article to fill up the spot where the editorial would have been. It was called "Raising Dogs in North Carolina."

Dickey refused to print it. Instead, he left the editorial space blank, with only a headline reading, "A Lament for Dr. Rose," and the word "CENSORED" underneath it in big, bold letters.

In addition, he sent a copy of the unprinted editorial to a Montgomery, Ala., newspaper.

Shortly afterwards, Gary Dickey was expelled from Troy State College for "willful and deliberate insubordination" in acting against the advice of President Adams and the faculty adviser.

Dickey decided to fight for his reinstatement, and the case of *Dickey vs. Alabama State Board of Education* came before the U. S. District Court in Alabama during the summer of 1967. Dickey had the backing of many groups in his battle for freedom of expression in a state-owned school. The Alabama affiliate of the ACLU filed a friend-of-the-court brief, along with the U. S. National Student Association, the U. S. Student Press Association, the American Association of University Professors and many other groups.

At the hearing, it was revealed that Troy State had a rule forbidding student editors to criticize the Governor of Alabama or the state legislature. If the editors did mention the state government at all, it had to be in a favorable light. This policy was known as "Adams' Rule."

In testimony, Sandra Rogers, the previous editor of *The Tripolitan,* recalled, "I went to see President Adams and asked [him] to explain the editorial policy of *The Tripolitan* to me. He told me that *The Tripolitan* could not criticize its owner and that Governor Wallace was, in effect, its owner. . . . [He] compared the paper with the buildings on campus, all of which, he said, were the property of the state."

When President Adams was called to testify, the following exchange took place:

> Question: Have you personally ever set a policy as to what could be printed in *The Tripolitan?*

> Dr. Adams: Generally, no—not specifically. I—I have said that I didn't think it was a good policy to criticize the Governor. Now, not Governor Wallace, but any Governor; the Governor is the President of our Board of Trustees, and I just don't think it is good policy to criticize the head of the—President of the Board of Trustees; I just don't think it is, and I have let that be known. . . ."

When asked by the Judge if the school policy also forbade writing favorable things about the governor and legislature, Dr. Adams replied: "Generally we just don't like to get into these—either favorable or unfavorable, because we—we—we have appropriations at stake; our livelihood depends upon—"

On September 8, 1967, the court ordered Troy State to readmit Gary Clinton Dickey, saying that just because a student went to a state-owned school, it did not mean he had to give up his constitutional right of freedom of expression. On the contrary, he is entitled to the same freedoms he would enjoy in a private school. The judge pointed out that the "insubordination" charge leveled against Dickey just cloaked the real grounds for his expulsion—his exercise of the right of academic and/or political expression.

It had also been argued that Dickey's readmission would threaten discipline in the college, but the court dismissed this as superficial, noting that it "completely ignores the greater damage to college students that will result from the imposition of intellectual restraints such as the 'Adams' Rule' in this case."

The American Civil Liberties Union believes that all student publications should enjoy full freedom of the press, without faculty advisers looking over the editors' shoulders, ready to veto anything they don't like. Prior censorship of this type is wrong because it prevents students from developing their own sense of responsibility and judgment, the ACLU feels. Students should write what they please, and face the possible consequences of their actions after publication, not before.

Then, editors who may be accused of untruthfulness, distortions or poor judgment by school officials should be granted full hearings before any effort is made to remove them from their editorial posts.

Cases involving freedom of the press or freedom of expression are part of the ACLU's everyday activities; the Union is expected to be concerned with these issues, whether they involve students or anyone else. But the Union has also taken on some unusual cases on behalf of students—like the time the New York affiliate of the ACLU found itself in court defending a girl who allegedly cheated on a test.

The girl, a 16-year-old high school student in New York City, was taking a New York State Regents examination one spring. In the middle of the test, she was caught with a "scratch paper" filled with notes.

When brought before the school's Acting Principal, Peter LoPiparo, the girl told him she had been cramming very hard earlier in the day, and after the test started, she had scribbled down everything she could remember on a piece of paper. She said she had written all the notes during the first half hour of the test.

The principal didn't believe her. He made her copy her own scratch sheet as fast as she could, but after 20 minutes she wasn't even a quarter of the way through. Then the principal quizzed her for two hours until finally the hysterical girl broke down and confessed. She had to sign a statement saying "I cheated."

The next day, the student retracted her statement, but it was too late. She got a zero on the test, and was barred from taking any more Regents examinations. This meant that she could not go to college, as she had planned.

The girl appealed to the New York Civil Liberties Union for help, and the Union agreed that the methods used to make her confess were not in keeping with the democratic processes. The NYCLU then sued for a reversal of the decision.

They won their case. A Queens Supreme Court Justice ruled that the girl had been denied "due process of law" by the state education department. The court pointed out that the penalties for cheating on a Regents exam were so severe that students should have some legal protection. The education department should have held a hearing at which the student "might defend herself with the assistance of counsel," the court declared.

Over the years, the American Civil Liberties Union has come to the aid of students so often that it has developed what amounts to a "student bill of rights." The guiding idea behind it is that if students are to be well trained in the democratic processes, they must be free to participate in the school and the community with rights "broadly analogous to those of adult citizens." This means they must have "freedom of expression, of assembly, of petition and of conscience, and to due process and equal treatment under the law."

More specifically, it means that schools should uphold the following principles:

- That no student should suffer any hurt or penalty for any idea he expresses while participating in class or school activities;
- That students in their schools have the right to live under "rule by law" rather than "rule by personality," mean-

ing that rules and regulations should be in writing, not subject to the whims of school officials;
- A recognition that freedom implies the right to make mistakes and that students must sometimes be allowed to act in ways which are predictably unwise so long as their acts are not dangerous to life or property;
- That no student should be denied an education or penalized because of his dress or grooming; as long as a student's appearance does not *in fact* disrupt classes, it should be of no concern to the school;
- That no student should suffer from racial or religious discrimination, either in the classroom or in extra-curricular activities such as social or athletic clubs; and that no student should have to salute the flag or recite any pledge of allegiance if it is against his religion or beliefs;
- That no student should be denied an education because of marriage or pregnancy.

These are just some of the many principles set down by the ACLU in its pamphlet *Academic Freedom in the Secondary Schools*. The ACLU emphasizes that students' rights should not be curbed without a compelling reason, such as one that presents a *clear and immediate danger* to the health and safety of others, or a serious disruption of classes.

As the ACLU says, "A school which does not respect civil liberties has failed the community, its students and itself." And the Supreme Court, in the *Gault* case, declared: ". . . Neither the Fourteenth Amendment nor the Bill of Rights is for adults alone."

[9]
HELPING THE OPPRESSED

Women

One week in March 1970, *Newsweek* magazine ran a cover story entitled, "Women in Revolt," which was all about the Women's Liberation Movement. In order to find a woman who could write this important article, *Newsweek* had to go outside its own staff. The magazine did not have any female news writers of its own.

That same week, 46 women staff members of *Newsweek* filed a suit against the magazine, charging that it systematically discriminated against them in its hiring and promotion policies, and had forced women "to assume a subsidiary role simply because they are women." They charged that such policies violated federal, state and city laws barring job discrimination on account of sex.

Representing the *Newsweek* women in their suit was Eleanor Holmes Norton, who at that time was Assistant Legal Director of the American Civil Liberties Union.

Mrs. Norton criticized *Newsweek* for having excluded women from writing jobs. She noted that there were more than 50 male writers on the magazine, but only one woman. Also, the magazine excluded women from jobs as correspondents, and rarely promoted them above the level of Assistant Editor. Training programs were reserved almost exclusively for men. Women were excluded from *Newsweek*'s Top of the Week luncheons, periscope panels and the campus speaker program.

"Indeed," Mrs. Norton said, "the entire atmosphere is one in which women are encouraged to think of themselves only as second-class employees. This is not because they lack competence or promise, but because they are women.

"*Newsweek* women possess impressive credentials. Graduates of such colleges and universities as Oxford, Radcliffe, Bryn Mawr and Berkeley, they hold academic honors, such as Phi Beta Kappa, and advanced degrees—including degrees in journalism. They have worked on newspapers, magazines and in government, and have published in journals such as the *New York Times Magazine, New York, Cosmopolitan* and *The Atlantic.*

"*Newsweek*'s caste system, however, relegates women with such credentials to research jobs almost exclusively and interminably," while men with inferior credentials often get the better jobs, Mrs. Norton said.

The 46 *Newsweek* women who joined in the lawsuit included almost all the researchers—the group most clearly discriminated against—as well as some reporters and a few other women directly involved in the editorial process. They appealed to the magazine's owner, Mrs. Katharine Graham, to step into the situation and eliminate the need to carry out the legal proceedings.

As Mrs. Norton said, "The *Newsweek* women believe that as a woman, Mrs. Graham has a particular responsibility to end discrimination against women at her magazine. I call upon her and her editors to negotiate this matter with me. . . . As a start, we ask for the immediate integration of the research staff and the opening of correspondence, writing and editing positions to women."

Helping the Oppressed

Eventually, the magazine agreed to alter its policies towards women, and the suit was settled out of court through negotiations between ACLU attorneys and *Newsweek* executives.

This was one of the many cases involving the rights of women that the ACLU has begun to handle in recent years. Few people even thought of women as an "oppressed" group until the early 1960s, when Betty Friedan came out with her book, *The Feminine Mystique,* and founded the National Organization of Women. This was the start of the nationwide Women's Liberation Movement, which has been calling attention to society's many prejudices against women.

Now, people have become far more aware of the fact that discrimination against women is woven into the very fabric of American society. It exists, in subtle ways, within the family structure itself, as well as in the schools, the business world and the government.

While the ACLU has always stood for equal rights for all, the organization recently took a close look at its own internal practices and came to the embarrassing conclusion that it, too, had been somewhat lax about placing women in policy-shaping positions.

At the 1970 ACLU Biennial Conference, the delegates passed a resolution noting that the organization had "underutilized" the potentialities and talents of women. The resolution pledged to "increase significantly" the representation of women on all policy-making bodies and committees of the ACLU. "Token representation will no longer be acceptable," the resolution stated. It also pledged that efforts would be made to open up all executive staff positions to women, including the executive directorship of the national office.

All resolutions passed by the delegates at the Biennial Conference are submitted to the ACLU Board of Directors, and become national policy if approved by the Board within 18 months. This resolution on women was passed by the Board.

In other Biennial Conference resolutions concerning women's rights, the delegates pledged to take legal action when necessary to guarantee the following principles:

- An end to all laws and policies that discriminate against women because of their marital status; a woman's marriage should never be a factor in terminating her employment or education, in awarding her scholarships or in determining her salary;
- A woman should have control over her own body, in cluding but not limited to the right to abortion, the right to birth control information and devices and the right to voluntary sterilization; nor should any woman be forced by law to restrict her child-bearing; these are part of every woman's right to the enjoyment of life, liberty and privacy;
- There should be no sex quotas in any co-educational college or university receiving government funds; all government scholarships should be awarded without regard to sex; dependency allowances should be granted on the same basis to men and women;
- Neither pregnancy nor motherhood should be a cause for involuntary termination of education or employment, or denial of opportunity for education or employment, if the woman's ability to perform is not impaired.

Three of these resolutions became official ACLU policy when they were approved by the national Board of Directors. But the resolution on women's control over their own bodies is still being considered, in the context of the whole population control issue rather than women's rights.

As part of its drive to secure equal rights for women, the ACLU filed a brief in the Supreme Court in May 1970 on behalf of Mrs. Ida Phillips, who was denied employment by the Martin Marietta Corporation because she was the mother of preschool-age children. The company hires men who are fathers of pre-school-age children, but discriminates against mothers. This, said the ACLU, is a violation of Title VII of the 1964 Civil Rights Act that forbade discrimination in hiring on account of sex.

In the Martin Marietta case, it was not a matter of discrimination based on sex alone; the corporation did hire women. It just didn't hire women with young children. The ACLU contended that this amounted to discrimination on the basis of "sex plus" an additional factor—in this instance, sex plus motherhood.

To allow this type of "sex plus" discrimination, the ACLU charged, will "not only jeopardize the entire anti-sex discrimination policy of the statute, but will seriously undermine all anti-discrimination laws."

If allowed to stand, "sex plus" exceptions could be used to upset many already established cases that had put an end to various types of sexual discrimination. For example, airlines could once again fire stewardesses who got married (sex "plus" marriage) or who reached age 32 (sex "plus" age).

In these types of cases, the woman's ability to do the job was not taken into consideration at all. The company merely said she would not be a good employee because of her sex "plus" some other arbitrary factor.

But the laws against discrimination require that people be considered as *individuals*, and not as part of any racial, religious or sexual class.

"To be judged as a member of a sub-class of women (those with preschool-age children) is still to be judged as a member of a class," the ACLU charged. "The discriminatory effect of the stereotyped assumption in Martin Marietta's policy is no different from the discriminatory effect of a stereotyped assumption about blacks or Jews; the latter is simply more obvious. . . .

"It is possible, of course, that Martin Marietta's policy is based on its feeling that mothers of preschool-age children *should not* work, not that they would be poor workers. But Title VII guarantees that women themselves, not their employers, retain the right to define the nature and extent of their responsibility to their children. . . . Despite the tradition—and the current mass media image—of a sexual division of labor in which women stay home, assuming the responsibility for housework and child care, and men work, assuming responsibility for monetary support, today not even a majority of American families fit this pattern."

There are 4.1 million mothers of preschool-age children in the United States, and a large percentage of them are part of the nation's labor force. In almost 40 percent of all U. S. families, women contribute to the financial support. To deny employment to any group of working women could create poverty in many families, the ACLU stated.

In January 1971, the Supreme Court handed down a decision in the case upholding the ACLU position. The Court ruled unanimously that the Civil Rights Act of 1964 forbids "one hiring policy for women and another for men," when both are parents of preschool-age children.

The ACLU is also involved in several cases dealing with discrimination against women in the armed services. In one case, an unmarried Navy enlisted woman was dismissed for "sexual immorality" after she had a miscarriage at her naval base. Her commanding officer said that if the Navy condoned unwed pregnancy, it would result in the lowering of "moral standards set for women in the Navy."

However, the ACLU pointed out that Navy men are not dismissed for fathering children out of wedlock. This "double standard" violates the Fourteenth Amendment's guarantee of equal protection of the laws, the ACLU charged.

In another case of this nature, a 26-year-old unmarried Air Force nurse who gave birth to a baby is fighting the Air Force's attempt to discharge her. Under Air Force regulations, women on active duty who become pregnant or give birth to a child are liable for immediate discharge. But with the help of ACLU lawyers, the nurse went to court and succeeded in blocking the discharge temporarily. The ACLU plans to take this case up to the Supreme Court, if necessary.

Among the many fields in which women are discriminated against is athletics. This begins at the elementary school level, where so many schools emphasize physical activity for boys but do not stress it for girls. In high schools and colleges, the teams that attract attention and draw the crowds are *boys'* teams; girls' teams, whether in basketball, softball or other sports, are often ridiculed.

But this attitude, too, is beginning to change. Recently, women fought for—and won—the right to be professional jockeys and to race alongside men jockeys in the major horse races around the country.

In 1970, the New York Civil Liberties Union took on the

case of a 16-year-old tennis player, Phyllis Graber, who was prevented from playing on her Jamaica High School team solely because she was a girl. The school had a boys' tennis team, but no girls' team, so she couldn't play at all. Therefore, she could not compete for a tennis scholarship, as she had hoped.

The coach of the boys' team, Ronald Ettus, said that Miss Graber was as good as any of the boys, and that he would have liked to have her on the team. "She would have made the team last year if she had been allowed to," he said. "The boys on the team had no objection to her playing at all."

However, the Public School Athletic League (PSAL) in New York City does not allow girls to compete against boys in athletics. In fact, the PSAL doesn't even let girls compete against girls. There is no inter-scholastic competition among girls at all in New York City high schools, in any sport. There will be soon, according to the PSAL, but the teams just haven't been organized yet.

Meanwhile, Miss Graber is being denied any opportunity to play high school tennis. In filling a formal complaint with the New York City Commission on Human Rights, Ira Glasser, Executive Director of the New York Civil Liberties Union said:

> The facts in this case make it clear that the Board of Education's policy prohibiting Miss Graber from playing on the tennis team is like prohibiting her from playing because she is Jewish. Her religion is no indication of her ability, and in this case, neither is her sex.
>
> Miss Graber is a serious tennis player. She has been taking lessons since she was nine years old, and she is hopeful of winning a tennis scholarship to attend college . . .

Helping the Oppressed [159]

Nevertheless, she has been prevented from competing—despite her ability—simply because PSAL rules do not permit it.

Mr. Glasser declared that the New York City Board of Education should not be allowed to spend public money for the support of athletics in a way that discriminated against one group, namely girls.

Subsequently, the Human Rights Commission upheld Miss Graber's complaint, so that girls may now compete with boys in non-contact sports such as tennis, track or swimming.

The Mentally Ill

In 1950, Alfred Curt von Wolfersdorf was arrested and charged with murder. He was then 66 years old, and had no previous criminal record. The only evidence linking him to the crime was the testimony of a co-defendant, who told several different versions of what happened at the time of the killing. In one version, he said that von Wolfersdorf had actually pulled the trigger. In another version, he said that von Wolfersdorf had supplied the gun, but was several miles away when the murder took place. In a third version, he said that he himself had pulled the trigger because von Wolfersdorf had forced him to.

Von Wolfersdorf denied all of these stories. He repeatedly declared he was innocent, and requested and took a lie detector test to prove it. He wanted to stand trial but, on the petition of the District Attorney, he was found mentally incompetent to stand trial and was committed to Matteawan State Hospital for the criminally insane. He was to be held there until he became competent.

Twenty years later, Alfred Curt von Wolfersdorf was still

being held in Matteawan—in criminal custody—even though he had never been convicted of a crime and never had a trial.

The state's case against von Wolfersdorf had been very weak to begin with. There wasn't a shred of real evidence against him. The charges rested solely on the word of his co-defendant, a very unstable man who was tried, convicted and executed in 1953.

Once this co-defendant was executed, the state no longer had any case at all against von Wolfersdorf. Nevertheless, it continued to hold him in a hospital for the "criminally" insane under the guise that he would someday be judged competent and would then be tried.

On 18 separate occasions, without the help of a lawyer, von Wolfersdorf demanded that he be brought to trial or that the criminal charges against him be dropped. His demands were ignored by the state and federal courts.

Writing about this in *Civil Liberties in New York,* the monthly publication of the NYCLU, Bruce J. Ennis said:

> Shortly after I became director of the Civil Liberties and Mental Illness Project, I received a letter from von Wolfersdorf requesting help. . . . The case was so old that it took my assistants, Loren Siegel and Lewis Novod, four months and numerous trips to Matteawan and the archives of the *Poughkeepsie Journal* before we were sure of the facts. I then tried, unsuccessfully, to persuade the District Attorney and the state courts to dismiss the indictment. Finally, having "exhausted" the state remedies which so often exist more in theory than in practice, I was able to file a federal habeas corpus petition.
>
> The question could be simply stated: Let us suppose a (presumably) innocent man is charged with a crime. Let

us suppose also that he is incompetent to prove his innocence. Can he constitutionally be held, under criminal auspices, for twenty years?

Judge Marvin E. Frankel said no. He ordered von Wolfersdorf released from criminal custody for three main reasons:

1. Criminal confinement of a presumably innocent man—merely because he is insane—is a "cruel and unusual punishment" for the "status" of being mentally ill. Thus, it violates the Eighth Amendment;
2. Incompetent defendants can only be held in criminal custody *temporarily;* long-term criminal hospitalization of a presumably innocent man is a violation of due process of law;
3. Incompetent defendants have as much right as competent ones to the Sixth Amendment's guarantee of a speedy trial.

The New York Civil Liberties Union felt that this last point was most important, for it was the first ruling that applied the speedy trial guarantees to an incompetent defendant.

The von Wolfersdorf case was just one example of the ACLU's growing interest in protecting the legal rights of mentally ill people. They, too, are among America's "disinherited," for they have enjoyed few legal protections in the past. Society generally just wants to get them out of the way and forget about them, so it has not been overly concerned about their rights. Even where they have not committed any criminal acts, and are not at all likely to do so, the mentally ill are often confined against their will, like criminals.

The New York Civil Liberties Union is challenging the

state's Mental Hygiene Law, which allows for 15-day confinement of "any person alleged to be in need of immediate observation, care or treatment for mental illness." Under this law, the person does not necessarily have to be dangerous, and the allegations against him may be made by anyone, solely on the basis of a rumor. The accused person cannot legally contest his confinement until after he is already confined.

The New York law does provide for immediate examination of the patient by a staff physician to see if the patient is "in need of immediate observation, care and treatment for mental illness." Even if the doctors decide that he is, the patient may "demand release at any time," and receive a prompt legal hearing to protest the doctors' decision. But during the whole procedure, the burden is on the patient to prove why he should not be detained.

The New York Civil Liberties Union contends that such commitment in a mental hospital is unconstitutional unless the patient is "imminently dangerous to himself or others," or if some type of "emergency" justifies his confinement. Otherwise, the NYCLU charges, the state does not have sufficient reason to justify taking away a person's liberty.

The American Civil Liberties Union is helping to bring another case of this type to the Supreme Court. The Court is being asked to rule for the first time on the constitutional rights of mental patients under *civil* commitment.

The particular case in question involves a Florida man who has been claiming for 10 years that he should be released from a state civil mental institution because he is no longer mentally ill. The ACLU has filed a friend-of-the-court brief in support of his petition, claiming that the man had been put away without "due process of law."

The ACLU contends that persons must not be deprived of

Helping the Oppressed [163]

their due process rights merely because the proceedings against them are called "civil" rather than "criminal," since a civil commitment deprives them of liberty just as much as a criminal commitment. The right of due process includes:

- The right to a lawyer, assigned by the court if necessary;
- The right to liberty unless the state can prove the need for confinement "beyond a reasonable doubt";
- The assumption that the burden of proof lies with the state rather than with the accused.

As of now, most people who are confined in mental institutions do not have such "due process" rights, and the ACLU is trying to see that they get them. The ACLU also contends that the mentally ill are entitled to periodic judicial review and to adequate psychiatric treatment. If such treatment cannot cure them, but they present no danger to themselves or others, the state should release them, the ACLU contends. However, the Union is making a further study of this matter. Other studies have shown that when hospitals release mental patients who have no prior arrest records, they are even less likely than most people to commit crimes. Thus, the ACLU says, the general assumption that the mentally ill must be removed from society because they are dangerous is not supported by the evidence.

Homosexuals

Homosexuals have been among the most oppressed groups in American society. Until recent times, social ostracism of homosexuals was so severe that many of them felt obliged to keep their homosexuality a secret from their employers, landlords, fellow workers or anyone else in the "straight" world. If they were so obviously homosexual that it couldn't be hidden, they became society's outcasts.

But the 1960s were a time when *all* oppressed groups began to assert their rights, and in this respect, homosexuals were no different. Homosexuals began demanding the right to live as freely and openly as anyone else, without fear of losing their jobs or being evicted because of their sexual preferences. More and more often, they began going to court to challenge discriminatory practices against them.

The American Civil Liberties Union has aided them in their struggle for the right to live and work like other people, and has brought two cases involving homosexuals before the Supreme Court. Both cases challenge the constitutionality of federal laws that restrict homosexuals' right to hold certain types of jobs.

In the first case, Robert Adams had been working for a private firm as an electrical technician for five years. During this time, he held a security clearance from the government allowing him access to classified materials.

At his employer's request, Mr. Adams applied for a Top Secret clearance. While being interviewed in regard to his application, Mr. Adams freely admitted that he was a homosexual. Because of this, not only was he denied Top Secret clearance, but his original security clearance was revoked. He was forced to take a leave of absence from his job.

In this case, the government had decided that it was not in the national interest for Mr. Adams to have access to classified information—despite the fact that there was no sign that he had ever misused any classified material during his years on the job. But the government was acting on the common assumption that homosexuals are more susceptible than most people to blackmail, and therefore are not good security risks.

In the second case, Richard L. Schlegel was employed for over 11 years as an Administrative Officer with the Department of the Army. As in Mr. Adams' case, Mr. Schlegel's superiors asked him to apply for a Top Secret clearance. After he did, it was learned that he was under investigation by the government for participation in homosexual activities. Because of this, Mr. Schlegel was removed from his job for "immoral and indecent conduct."

In bringing these cases to the Supreme Court, the ACLU stated that both Adams and Schlegel had been deprived of their due process rights under the Fifth Amendment. The organization also declared that the government could not deny a security clearance to an individual or dismiss a federal employee *solely* on the grounds that they had engaged in private homosexual activity with a consenting adult.

The ACLU cited several scholarly studies refuting the assumption that homosexuals were security risks because they were more likely than others to be blackmailed. The ACLU also charged that the government was discriminating unjustly against "an already persecuted minority" when it closed off jobs to people solely because of their homosexuality.

In another case involving homosexuals, the Minnesota Civil Liberties Union went to court to stop the University of Minnesota from denying a library job to a fully qualified person solely because he was a homosexual.

The young man had been chosen by the University to head the cataloging division of the library at the St. Paul campus. The Board of Regents must formally approve such employment, but it refused to do so after local newspapers reported that the man in question had applied for a license to marry another man.

The Board felt that "his personal conduct, as represented in the public and university news media, is not consistent with the best interests of the University."

The Minnesota CLU sued in the man's behalf, and won its case in the Federal District Court. The Court said that when the University denied the man a job, it violated his right under the Fourteenth Amendment to be free from discrimination, as well as his First Amendment right of free speech.

The Court declared "there was no attempt to show that [the man's] homosexual tendencies might affect the performance of his duties or his efficiency as a librarian.

". . . Though by current standards many persons characterize a homosexual as engaging in 'immoral conduct,' 'indecent' and 'disgraceful,' it seems clear that to . . . reject an applicant for public employment it must be shown that there is an observable relationship between efficiency in the job and homosexuality.

". . . What he does in his private life, as with other employees, should not be his employer's concern unless it can be shown to affect in some degree his efficiency in the performance of his duties. . . ."

The ACLU couldn't agree more.

[10]
THE ACLU TODAY AND TOMORROW

The ACLU's activities over the past 10 years have mirrored the concerns of America as a whole during the chaotic, turbulent and troubled decade of the 1960s.

During the previous decade—the somber 1950s, when America's youth was a "silent generation" rather than a liberated, activist one, and adults were obsessed with fears of a communist conspiracy—the work of the ACLU was far different. Then, no book about civil liberties would have dared come out without lengthy chapters on the rights of citizens in loyalty-security investigations; the constitutionality of loyalty oaths; past membership in "subversive" organizations; the right not to be judged on the basis of guilt by association; the right to hold a job despite one's political views; and other civil liberties issues that cropped up as a result of fears that communists were undermining the country. These issues monopolized the ACLU's activities then, for communism was the overriding concern of the 1950s, particularly during the first half of the decade.

But by the 1960s, the "communist menace" had faded into the background, at least as a domestic issue. Other civil liberties issues became far more prominent, and even though the ACLU still handled a good many loyalty-security cases, these no longer made up the bulk of the organization's work. The major civil liberties issues of the 1960s grew out of the opposition to the

Vietnam War, the ever more militant drive for black rights and the intense desire on the part of the young to change the established order and end the injustices done to all the oppressed groups.

In the 1960s, too, the country began to shed many of its outworn customs and restraints, and there was a strong demand for greater freedom. Movies and books reflected a much freer attitude towards such subjects as sex, nudity and obscenity. Young people, in particular, discarded traditional clothes and hairstyles, and developed their own "look." More seriously, they began questioning the basic values of American society, and became far more skeptical about the importance of getting a "good job," becoming a "success" and accumulating material possessions. Minority groups that had passively accepted their second-class status for so long awoke with loud and insistent demands for their rights. There was a new emphasis on the worth of the individual in relation to the government.

The 1960s were a time of change—and a time when those who wanted the change were locked in battle with those who didn't want it. All too often, these battles became violent, erupting in the universities, the urban ghettos and the streets.

But the battles that accomplished the most took place in the legislatures and the courtrooms. The Supreme Court, under the leadership of former Chief Justice Earl Warren, led the way in promoting a spirit of change and a new concern for individual rights and freedoms.

The ACLU and other civil liberties groups found that they were winning many important legal victories involving freedom of speech and expression, the right of privacy, conscientious objection, freedom of assembly, greater protection for those accused of crimes and the like. In many instances, these cases involved new interpretations and expansions of old rights. For example, those who got into trouble for tampering with the American flag or violating school dress codes claimed the right of *symbolic* free speech—that is, expressing their feelings and opinions through symbolic gestures rather than actual speech. In many cases, the courts upheld their right. Also, many of the basic rights that adults have always enjoyed were extended for the first time to children or students within the schools.

As different minority groups began asserting their rights, the ACLU became involved in the civil liberties aspects of their struggles, too. The Union not only intensified its efforts on behalf of blacks, but also took on cases for migrant workers and other oppressed groups that had not raised their voices before, such as women, homosexuals, the mentally ill and prisoners.

At the close of the 1960s, the ACLU was looking into other issues that have also become part of our times—the drug problem, the population explosion and threats to the environment.

At the 1970 ACLU Biennial Conference, delegates approved the following policy in regard to the use of drugs:

- An individual has the right to use his own body as he wishes, and this right includes the use and possession of narcotics;
- The use and possession of drugs is not per se a crime, and should invoke no criminal penalties; however, *conduct* resulting from the use or possession of drugs may invoke civil or criminal penalties;
- The government may regulate, including by means of government monopoly, the sale of drugs;
- Compulsory treatment or imprisonment of drug *users* is a violation of civil liberties;
- All of these resolutions apply *only to adults;* no position

is taken on the right of juveniles to use or possess drugs other than to recommend that a comprehensive study of the rights of juveniles in this area be undertaken.

On the subject of the environment, the ACLU was split over whether the ecological threat to human survival could be viewed as a civil liberties concern. Some ACLU affiliates had launched suits in this area, while others felt that this subject was outside the realm of the ACLU's functions, and should better be left to other organizations.

The majority of delegates at the Biennial Conference felt that it was an appropriate field for ACLU activity, stating that "a habitable environment is an absolute precondition for the existence of civil liberties," and "the right to a habitable environment is itself a substantive civil liberty."

The delegates said that in any instance where government or private activity threatens the habitable environment, the people in that area should "be entitled to access to public records relevant to the danger," and have the right to be heard in administrative and judicial hearings on the matter.

The delegates also felt that "the ACLU should become actively involved in developing these rights and in cases and legislation presenting environmental issues."

The Biennial Conference resolutions must be approved by the ACLU Board of Directors before they become official ACLU policy.

The split within the ACLU over whether or not the threat to the environment is a proper civil liberties concern is not the only internal dispute of this nature.

The ACLU has gone into many new areas over the past decade, such as welfare rights, the rights of students in high schools and the rights of various oppressed groups. Some members feel that these are not strictly civil liberties matters, but rather are matters of social reform. Even stronger differences of opinion have arisen over the Vietnam War, particularly over the constitutionality of the draft and the right of conscientious objection to a *particular* war.

In all these disputes, the majority eventually favored expanding the ACLU's role, while the minority fought to remain within the Union's traditional limits.

The split was particularly sharp within the New York Civil Liberties Union, which is one of the ACLU's most activist, expansionist affiliates. In a battle over the election of officers in 1970, the opposing viewpoints emerged very clearly. Taking the expansionist point of view was Sheldon Ackley, who was running for reelection as chairman of the NYCLU Board of Directors. He stated:

> I am disturbed that some members oppose the extension of rights to new groups just when the civil liberties of racial minorities, women, children and the impoverished hang in the balance. I am disturbed that some members oppose "political" activity by NYCLU just when our increased membership and legal successes give us a chance of legislative victories. I am disturbed that some members would restrict our support of the rights to dissent just when war, race and poverty impose conditions against which many wish to object publicly.
>
> I believe the NYCLU should continue its aggressive leadership in the struggle for civil liberties. I realize this sets it upon a collision course with forces, both governmental and private, that would repress those who seek

change and still those who dissent from official policies. But the confrontation is necessary, for on its outcome rests the future of liberty in the United States.

Among the insurgents opposing Mr. Ackley and his slate of nominees were Robert J. Christen and Monroe Lerner, who put forth the traditionalist viewpoint in a joint statement. They said:

"We must continue the unique 50-year-old ACLU tradition of uniting various viewpoints around our basic policy of defending the civil liberties of all. Our credibility should not be jeopardized by allowing ourselves to be partisan to every social and economic conflict that hits the front pages. We need not adopt the Cause in order to aggressively and effectively defend the rights of those advocating the Cause."

Another insurgent, Stanley Engelstein, agreed with this position, adding: "The growing tendency of the NYCLU to compromise civil libertarianism in the interest of 'just causes' endangers the cause of civil liberties. We need an impartial NYCLU that will not lose its credibility by partisan involvement in political struggles or generate internal division by advocating social and economic programs."

Mr. Ackley and his slate won reelection by a comfortable margin, 65-35, guaranteeing that the NYCLU would continue its expansionist trend.

The national ACLU has also been heading in an expansionist direction. Aryeh Neier, who led the NYCLU for five years and was largely responsible for its expanded activism, was elected executive director of the ACLU in September 1970, at the age of 33. He succeeded John de J. Pemberton, Jr., who had been the director for eight years.

The ACLU Today and Tomorrow

During his tenure, Mr. Pemberton had sought more active ACLU involvement in many areas, particularly in issues related to selective service. He resigned in order to return to the practice of law, where he could be a more direct advocate rather than an administrator.

Towards the end of the 1960s, the ACLU found itself up against new threats to civil liberties. The growing disruption and violence of the era, plus the alarming increase in crime, were creating loud demands for "law and order." President Nixon proposed a "safe streets" and "anti-crime" bill containing many provisions that the ACLU felt were clearly unconstitutional. Among these were a "preventive detention" act that would enable judges in federal courts to hold people accused of violent crimes in jail prior to their trial, and *not allow them out on bail*. This would be done in any case where the judge felt that if the suspect was out on the streets while awaiting trial, he would be likely to commit more crimes in the interim.

The ACLU has been waging an all-out fight against this proposed measure, and has helped form a National Committee Against Preventive Detention to educate the public about its dangers. Arthur Goldberg, former Supreme Court Justice and Ambassador to the United Nations, was named chairman of the committee. He called preventive detention "alien to the American concept of law enforcement" because it would "punish persons for actions which may take place in the future." He pointed out that the right of bail is required by the Eighth Amendment.

Another provision of the anti-crime bill—the "no-knock" clause—would allow federal narcotics agents to break into suspects' homes without any warning, and would even give them the right to make exploratory searches without search warrants.

Other provisions of the bill include compulsion of physical evidence, broader electronic surveillance and mandatory minimum sentences.

The ACLU's former Washington office director, Lawrence Speiser, called the total bill "a dreadful collection of police state measures."

The Union also campaigned very hard against a bill aimed at organized crime, which it felt would make "drastic incursions on the civil liberties of everyone—not just members of organized crime groups."

Among the most dangerous features of the bill, the ACLU felt, were the denial of the privilege against self-incrimination at hearings; the power given to courts to summarily imprison witnesses who refuse to testify for up to 36 months, without a jury trial; use of evidence obtained by methods that violate the Constitution; and special sentencing provisions permitting up to 30 years' imprisonment for loosely defined "dangerous special offenders."

The ACLU felt that a bill of this type would almost certainly be used against anti-draft and anti-war protestors, and radical and militant groups, as well as against organized crime groups.

To gather information about the growing number of radical groups, the government tried to subpoena journalists to testify about their confidential talks with members of these groups. The ACLU protested this as a violation of freedom of the press, and filed a friend-of-the-court brief in the case of Earl Caldwell, a reporter who was refusing to testify about information given to him in confidence by the Black Panthers.

The ACLU argued that enforcement of the subpoena would "destroy Mr. Caldwell's journalistic relationship with the Panthers and render it all but impossible for him to report on them in the future. All of us will be the poorer for this."

The ACLU also asserted that the press was protected against this type of action by the First Amendment because, as the Supreme Court stated in 1945, a free press "is essential to the welfare of the public."

In addition, the ACLU said the Panthers—like everyone else in the country—had a constitutional right of privacy in political association, and it was their privilege to speak anonymously.

However, there is a reverse side to the free press issue that the ACLU is also concerned about. At times, reporters may have information that could help a defendant at a trial. If they claimed the right to withhold this information as "confidential," it could result in a denial of due process of law for the defendant.

The 1960s were also a time when colleges and universities became embroiled in political turmoil. In many schools, student radicals staged demonstrations and seized buildings, in an attempt to force school administrators to comply with their demands for change. The ACLU's position regarding such acts is as follows:

"We believe in the right, and are committed to the protection of, all *peaceful* forms of protest, including mass demonstrations, picketing, rallies and other dramatic forms. But actions which deprive others of the opportunity to speak or be heard, involve takeovers of buildings that disrupt the educational process, incarceration of or assaults on persons, destruction of property and rifling of files, are anti-civil libertarian and incompatible with the nature and functions of educational institutions."

All too often in the 1960s, the police, state troopers or national guardsmen had to be summoned to schools to put down demonstrations. Sometimes bloody clashes took place, even when the demonstrations themselves may have been non-violent.

These confrontations between students and the police came to a tragic climax in 1970, when a number of students were killed and many were wounded at Jackson State College in Mississippi and Kent State University in Ohio.

At Kent, a large group of students were engaged in a peaceful demonstration when the National Guard—apparently ill-prepared to handle such a situation and reacting in fear—opened fire on the crowd. Four students were killed, including a girl who was just observing the melee from a distance.

In October 1970, the President's Commission on Campus Unrest, which investigated the episode thoroughly, reported that the Kent State shootings were "unnecessary, unwarranted and inexcusable."

However, a special Ohio State grand jury disagreed, declaring that all of the protestors, including "onlookers," were at least "morally" responsible for what happened. The grand jury issued indictments against 25 members of the Kent academic community, and concluded that the National Guardsmen were "honest and sincere" in their fear of bodily harm to themselves when they fired into the crowd.

The ACLU believes that the shootings at Kent State and the grand jury indictments of students and faculty were a shameful miscarriage of justice. To combat this, the ACLU has filed several lawsuits in connection with the Kent State tragedy. The Union declared:

> In the name of the law, public authorities have visited upon the Kent State University community a series of lawless actions. In the name of law, the American Civil Liberties Union urges that these public servants must be held legally accountable. For without this accounting, the rule of law will not endure.
>
> Kent is a reality in which four young men and women

were slain, nine were wounded, and every member of the community was denied his most fundamental liberties. Kent will also become a symbol. It may become a symbol of official lawlessness and the futility of attempts at lawful change. Or it may become a symbol of the return of law and renewed faith in a society in which liberty and life may endure. The ACLU is committed to law, to liberty and to life.

Among the lawsuits were the following:

- *Wrongful Death Case.* The ACLU has filed a $1 million federal damage suit charging Ohio officials with "reckless and wanton" actions in causing the death of Sandra Scheur, one of the slain students. The ACLU also charges the governor with inflammatory rhetoric, unnecessary use of the National Guard and improper control of the troops, including allowing them to carry and use loaded guns. Guard officials are charged with reckless failure to control the troops and ordering the shooting. The troops are charged with intentional and reckless shooting, and the President of Kent is charged with recklessly abandoning his campus to outside control.
- *National Guard Case.* The ACLU has filed a federal lawsuit to get a court determination of the conditions under which the National Guard may be called to Ohio campuses and the rules the troops must observe in performing their duties. Among other contentions, the ACLU says the premature use of the Guard at Kent inhibited the exercise of First Amendment rights and increased the risk of killing; in controlling civilian dis-

orders, troops should use non-lethal weapons and should know that they may not wantonly use deadly force.
- *Search and Seizure Case.* After the shootings in May, state, local and university police systematically searched every student room on the campus. These searches were all conducted without warrants. The ACLU has filed a federal lawsuit to prevent repetition of such searches and to compel return of the seized items (mostly such "weapons" as jackknives).
- *FBI Case.* The ACLU will sue the Attorney General of the United States, the director of the FBI and the Kent campus security officer for probing the political beliefs of students and faculty after the shootings. Dossiers were made on so-called radicals—that is, people who had engaged in peaceful demonstrations and meetings. Members of the academic community were quizzed about each other's political opinions, activities and associations. FBI undercover agents were planted on the campus as students.
- *Grand Jury.* The ACLU has called for a federal grand jury investigation to find out whether guardsmen, acting under cover of law, violated the constitutional rights of students and others, in violation of federal civil rights law.

In addition to these and other lawsuits, the ACLU is helping to defend members of the Kent academic community who were indicted by the Ohio State grand jury. The ACLU hopes that these Kent lawsuits—plus other suits arising from the killings at Jackson State, from bloody police actions at Portland State University and from National Guard brutality at the University of New Mexico—will help end the reckless use of force and bloodshed in suppressing student demonstrations.

The ACLU believes that the Nixon administration has been taking unduly repressive measures in its attempt to combat crime and radicalism. As Edward J. Ennis, Chairman of the ACLU, stated:

"The positions President Nixon and the Department of Justice have taken on preventive detention, wiretapping and searches are ominous signs of a disposition towards unconstitutional repression, which can be halted only by defending the civil liberties of those under attack, by alerting the public to the real danger in any government attempt to suspend freedoms and by encouraging the free exercise of legitimate civil liberties."

Sharing these fears of growing repression, *The New York Times* stated in an editorial:

> Under the guise of essential attacks on crime, police and investigatory powers are being sharpened for potential use against *political* offenders. Preventive detention is being advocated, when too many suspects are already imprisoned too long before being brought to trial. No-knock entry into private premises and the rifling of confidential records are being justified as weapons against narcotics.
>
> Political snooping has seriously jeopardized the confidentiality of income tax returns and diminished the privilege of reporters' files. Personal mail is increasingly subject to scrutiny.
>
> . . . There are those who say that the growing reliance on surveillance, with lines blurred between the legitimate

attack on crime and the illegitimate repression of dissent, is the price of America's role as a great power, but that is to misread the country's destiny. The nation's greatness springs from its dream of greater freedoms for all, not from a nightmare of restricted liberties for some. Today, no less than in earlier times of trouble, the Bill of Rights offers the best, perhaps the last, hope to carry the torch against the forces of dark suspicion and fear.

No one could agree with this more than the American Civil Liberties Union, whose single purpose over the last 50 years has been to "defend the whole Bill of Rights for everyone."

THE BILL OF RIGHTS

AMENDMENT 1

Congress shall make no law respecting an establishment of religion, or prohibiting the free exercise thereof; or abridging the freedom of speech, or of the press; or the right of the people peaceably to assemble, and to petition the Government for a redress of grievances.

AMENDMENT 2

A well regulated Militia, being necessary to the security of a free State, the right of the people to keep and bear Arms, shall not be infringed.

AMENDMENT 3

No Soldier shall, in time of peace be quartered in any house, without the consent of the Owner, nor in time of war, but in a manner to be prescribed by law.

AMENDMENT 4

The right of the people to be secure in their persons, houses, papers, and effects, against unreasonable searches and seizures, shall not be violated, and no Warrants shall issue, but upon probable cause, supported by Oath or affirmation, and particularly describing the place to be searched, and the persons or things to be seized.

AMENDMENT 5

No person shall be held to answer for a capital, or otherwise infamous crime, unless on a presentment or indictment of a Grand Jury, except in cases arising in the land or naval forces, or in the Militia, when in actual service in time of War or public danger; nor shall any person be subject for the same offence to be twice put in jeopardy of life or limb; nor shall be compelled in any criminal case to be a witness against himself, nor be deprived of life, liberty, or property, without due process of law; nor shall private property be taken for public use, without just compensation.

AMENDMENT 6

In all criminal prosecutions, the accused shall enjoy the right to a speedy and public trial, by an impartial jury of the State and district wherein the crime shall have been committed, which district shall have been previously ascertained by law, and to be informed of the nature and cause of the accusation; to be confronted with the witnesses against him; to have compulsory process for obtaining witnesses in his favor, and to have the Assistance of Counsel for his defence.

AMENDMENT 7

In Suits at common law, where the value in controversy shall exceed twenty dollars, the right of trial by jury shall be preserved, and no fact tried by a jury, shall be otherwise re-examined in any Court of the United States, than according to the rules of the common law.

AMENDMENT 8

Excessive bail shall not be required, nor excessive fines imposed, nor cruel and unusual punishments inflicted.

AMENDMENT 9

The enumeration in the Constitution, of certain rights, shall not be construed to deny or disparage others retained by the people.

AMENDMENT 10

The powers not delegated to the United States by the Constitution, nor prohibited by it to the States, are reserved to the States respectively, or to the people.

SUGGESTED FURTHER READINGS

Breckenridge, Adam Carlyle. *The Right to Privacy*. Lincoln, Nebraska: University of Nebraska Press, 1970.

Dorsen, Norman. *Frontiers of Civil Liberties*. New York: Random House, 1968.

Douglas, William O. *Freedom of the Mind*. New York: Doubleday, 1964.

Johnson, Donald. *The Challenge to American Freedoms—World War I and the Rise of the ACLU*. Kentucky: University of Kentucky Press, 1963.

Markmann, Charles Lamm. *The Noblest Cry; a History of the ACLU*. New York: St. Martin's Press, 1965.

McClellan, Grant S., editor. *Civil Rights*. (The Reference Shelf, Vol. 36, No. 6.) New York: H. W. Wilson Co., 1964.

Reitman, Alan, editor. *The Price of Liberty: Perspectives on Civil Liberties by Members of the ACLU*. New York: W. W. Norton & Co., 1968.

Roche, John P. *The Quest for the Dream*. New York: The Macmillan Company, 1963.

Way, H. Frank. *Liberty in the Balance*. New York: McGraw-Hill, 1964.

INDEX

Academic Freedom in the Secondary Schools (ACLU), 149
Ackley, Sheldon, 171-172
Adams, John, 16
Adams, Ralph, 144-146
Adams, Robert, 164, 165
Addams, Jane, 17
Agnew, Spiro, 21
American Civil Liberties Union
  black community and, 63-82;
  Black Panthers and, 79-80, 109;
  conservative political organizations and, 83-97; credit bureaus and, 114-118; *Dickey vs. Alabama State Board of Education* and, 143-146; *Ferrell vs. Dallas Independent School District,* 140-142; flag desecration cases and, 51-62; future of, 167-180; *Girouard vs. United States* and, 36; *Griswold vs. Connecticut* and, 10-12, 101; headquarters of, 12; history of, 16-25; homosexuals and, 163-166; Kent State University and, 176-178; the mentally ill and, 159-163; migrant workers and, 131-133; military service and, 27-50; Nation States Rights Party and, 84-91; *Oestereich vs. Selective Service Board No. 11* and, 45-46; *Olmstead vs. United States* and, 102-103; operations of, 22-25; pacificism and, 27-50; privacy, right to, and 99-118; *Richards vs. Thurston* and, 142; the Right, and 83-97; *Rosado vs. Wyman* and, 130-131; routine cases of, examples, 23-25; Scopes trial and, 18; Scottsboro case and, 65-66; students and, 135-149; surveillance of citizens and, 99-118; *Tinker vs. Des Moines, Iowa School Board* and

137-140; today, 9-25, 167-180; Vietnam and, 21-22, 27-28, 38-50; welfare recipients and, 119-131; women's liberation movement and, 151-159; youth and, 135-149
Apthecker, Bettina, 144

Baldwin, Roger, 17, 22, 38
Barnett, Ross, 97
Bartlett, Dewey F., 107
Belloni, Robert C., 142
Birth of a Nation, 63-64
Black, Hugo, 101
Black, Jr., Fred B., 104
Black Justice (ACLU), 65
Brandeis, Louis D., 87, 102-103
Brennen, William, 129
Bronstein, Alvin, 68-69
Brown, W. P., 52
Brown vs. The Board of Education, 20-21

Caldwell, Earl, 174
Calley, Lt. William, 14-15
Carmichael, Stokely, 144
Carpenter, George A., 32-35
Carroll, Joseph, 86-91
Carswell, G. Harrold, 12-13
Chavez, Cesar, 132-133
Civil Liberties (ACLU), 71

Cohen, Jules, 94
Coxe, Spencer, 93-95, 143

Darrow, Clarence, 17, 18
Darwin, Charles, 18
Debs, Eugene V., 16
Dewey, John, 17
Dickey, Gary Clinton, 144-146
Dickey vs. Alabama State Board of Education, 143-146
Douglas, William O., 44, 45-46, 101, 102

Eckhardt, Christer, 138
Eisenhower, Dwight D., 95
Engelstein, Stanley, 172
Ennis, Bruce J., 160
Ennis, Edward J., 179
Epton, William, 91
Ernst, Morris, 17
Ervin, Sam, 106, 109-110
Ettus, Ronald, 158
Evans, Dale, 58

Faubus, Orval, 120
Feminine Mystique, The (Friedan), 153
Ferrell, Phillip, 140-142
Ferrell vs. Dallas Independent School District, 140-142
Fitch, David, 60-62

Index

Flane, Joseph, 53
Fortas, Abe, 88
Fox, John Brackenbrough, 86
Frankel, Marvin E., 161
Frankfurter, Felix, 17
Friedan, Betty, 153
Fuller, Louis, 121

Garbus, Martin, 120, 123-125
Gault, Gerald, 135-136, 149
George III (king of England), 113
Girouard vs. United States, 36
Glasser, Ira, 158-159
Goldberg, Arthur, 173
Goodman, Walter, 121
Graber, Martha, 30-31
Graber, Phyllis, 158-159
Graham, Mrs. Katherine, 152
Griffin, James, 57
Griswold vs. Connecticut, 10-12, 101

Hague, Frank, 18
Hays, Arthur Garfield, 18
Hershey, Gen. Lewis B., 44, 46
Hitler, Adolf, 27, 37
Hoffman, Abie, 51, 58
Holmes, Oliver Wendell, 35, 87
Hoover, J. Edgar, 32, 103

Houston, Charles H., 67
Hubner, Mrs. Betsy, 57-58
Hughes, Richard, 81

Jarvis, Paul, 140
Johnson, Lyndon B., 39, 104
Joyce, James, 19

Kaplowitz, Leo, 81
Karpatkin, Marvin, 42
Kerner, Otto, 110
King, Reuben, 123
King, Jr., Martin Luther, 112

Laird, Melvin, 15
Lindbergh, Charles A., 53
LoPiparo, Peter, 147
Lykken, David T., 9-10

Madison, James, 47
Malave, Juan, 127
Marx, Karl, 18
McCarthy, Eugene, 111
McCarthy, Joseph, 20, 84, 95
McIntire, Rev. Carl, 92-95
Meredith, James, 59
Mikva, Abner J., 110
Mitchell, John, 21, 104-105

Neier, Aryeh, 172

Nixon, Richard M., 12, 39, 43, 104, 173, 179
Norton, Eleanor Holmes, 88-91, 151-152
Novod, Lewis, 160
Noyd, Capt. Dale, 40-44

Oestereich vs. Selective Service Board No. 11, 45-46
Olmstead vs. United States, 102-103
Oxfeld, Emil, 96

Pemberton, Jr., John de, 42, 49, 172-173
Phillips, Mrs. Ida, 155

Ramos, Miriam, 127
Ratliff, John, 45
Reitman, Alan, 25
Resor, Stanley R., 110
Richards, Robert, 142
Richards vs. Thurston, 142
Rockwell, George Lincoln, 84, 96
Rogers, Roy, 58
Rogers, Sandra, 145
Rosado, Julia, 131
Rosado vs. Wyman, 130-131
Rose, Dr. Frank, 144

Sheppard, Dr. Samuel, 15

Schlegel, Richard L., 165
Schwimmer, Rosika, 31-36
Scopes, John Thomas, 18
Siegal, Loren, 160
Smith, Mrs. Sylvester, 120-126
Snell, Geraldine, 127
Speiser, Lawrence, 61-62, 174
Spock, Dr. Benjamin, 27
Stancil, Jacquelyn, 122
Stapp, Mary, 125
Stark, Matthew, 9
Stevenson III, Adlai E., 110
Stokes, Rose Pastor, 17
Street, Sidney, 58-59

Tarmann, Vera Ann, 137
Thomas, Norman, 17
Tinker, Mary Beth, 137-140
Tinker vs. Des Moines, Iowa, School Board, 137-140
Tremain, Russell, 52-53

Ulysses (Joyce), 19

Von Wolfersdorf, Alfred Curt, 159-161

Wallace, George, 89, 90, 92, 145, 146
Warren, Earl, 95, 168

Index

Webb, Stephen, 140-141
Westin, Alan, 116-117
Wheelen, Gen. Earl, 144
Williams, George Washington, 86

Williams, William E., 122
Wulf, Melvin, 61-62, 89, 140

Zenman, William, 89

ABOUT THE AUTHOR

Barbara Habenstreit was born and grew up in New York City. She attended the Bronx High School of Science and City College, where she majored in government and put out the student newspaper, *The Campus*. After graduation she worked as a reporter and editor for a weekly newspaper in the city and as a writer for a national trade publication. She received a master's degree in political science and international relations from Long Island University, then taught at the University for a short time before becoming a freelance writer. She is married to Abraham Habenstreit, assistant to the President at Staten Island Community College of the City University. They have a son, David, and a daughter, Shelly, and live in the Fort Greene section of Brooklyn.